WILL YOUR ANCH

Cover photo of Stromness – photo credit to Steve Roden Images (steveroden.net)

Scripture quotations taken from The Holy Bible, New International Version © copyright 1973, 1978, 1984, 2011 by Biblica Inc. Used by permission. All rights reserved worldwide.

Good Good Father, song by Pat Barrett © 2014 Capital CMG

The Wild Ones, Nate Johnston, Destiny Image © 2021

Why Men Hate Going to Church, David Murrow © 2011

WILL YOUR ANCHOR HOLD

WHAT OTHERS ARE SAYING

"I've known Ricky for 25 years, this is the inspiring story of his faith, friendship and fatherhood in the midst of ordinary, everyday life. His real and raw journey speaks to us of a bigger miracle, in which we can all discover God's best for our lives as men".

Rev Simon Dennis (Lead Pastor, Sheddocksley Baptist Church, Aberdeen)

"Ricky is a man who wears his heart very much on his sleeve. His book will take you through the highs, but also the honest lows of a life fully lived. Much of his adult life has been devoted to living out his Christian faith in a time where society values materialism and consumerism rather than Christian integrity. Read this book to walk in his shoes for a short while and you might just look at your own values and beliefs in a different light."

Gregor Howitt (Church advisor, Aberdeen)

"Ricky has seen his life transformed by coming into a personal relationship with Jesus Christ. His story highlights the ups and downs of life we often all face, and despite the challenges he continues to steadfastly pursue God's leading for his life. An example to us all of perseverance in action. I hope others on this journey will be encouraged by his testimony and life story"

Jim Grimmer (Found and Business Partner, P3 Business Care CIC)

WILL YOUR ANCHOR HOLD

INTRODUCTION	
CHAPTER 1	THE STROMNESS BOY
CHAPTER 2	RUNNING EVERYWHERE
CHAPTER 3	BEHIND THE SMILE
CHAPTER 4	FINDING MY IDENTITY
CHAPTER 5	LIFE IS AN ADVENTURE
CHAPTER 6	THE GAME CHANGER
CHAPTER 7	OUT OF CONTROL
CHAPTER 8	NO ONE LOVES LIKE JOANNE
CHAPTER 9	THE BATTLE
CHAPTER 10	THE EVER-GROWING FAMILY
CHAPTER 11	ON THE MOVE
CHAPTER 12	A SEASON OF GROWTH
CHAPTER 13	FAMILY FIRST
CHAPTER 14	ALFORD
CHAPTER 15	THE CALL
CHAPTER 16	STILL IN THE GAME
EPILOGUE	THE JOURNEY GOES ON…..

WILL YOUR ANCHOR HOLD

ACKNOWLEDGEMENTS

I want to dedicate this book to my family, who are my constant support and encouragement through the rollercoaster of life. I believe every person has a story to share, and by writing my story I hope and pray that this can encourage even just one person. My life, in some ways, has been ordinary, but has been impacted by an extraordinary God, without Him this book would never have been possible.

A big shout out to my friend Simon who helped me get this book ready to print.

Finally, to all the men and women who have impacted my life in ways you'll never know – thankyou from the bottom of my heart.

WILL YOUR ANCHOR HOLD

INTRODUCTION

In this book you can journey with me from my upbringing in the beautiful town of Stromness in the Orkney islands to the big city of Aberdeen, and beyond to the 'shire where I now live.

Even at a young age I always felt that I had a different spirit, one that would often get me in trouble as a youth. However, with God in the equation, I received a spirit that can be moulded to break down the ordinary lifestyle. Once I discovered who I was in Christ then my true identity was revealed.

Please enjoy this story about an ordinary boy who looked to have it all as a youngster, but hid his troubles behind a big smile. We all have a story to tell, this one is transparent, open and unashamedly honest. From the lows of losing family members, to the multiple car crashes, to marrying my beautiful wife Joanne within nine months of meeting, and going on to have five amazing kids.

Hopefully you will see how God can take an ordinary man and use him way beyond his natural abilities. Having a different spirit combined with faith, life is one great adventure, so let's begin…

WILL YOUR ANCHOR HOLD

CHAPTER 1 - THE STROMNESS BOY

Born in Aberdeen on 25th March 1969, my parents were delighted to have boy number three, yes, I was the youngest. My two older brothers were ten and three years older than me, so being the youngest was for me always a strength, and I loved being the baby of the family.

We moved from Aberdeen to Stromness Orkney in 1970, so obviously I had no recollection of anything Aberdeen. To this day people tell me that I am not a true Orcadian due to the place of my birth, but I can truly say that Orkney will always be number one in my heart : you can take the boy out of Orkney, but you cannot take Orkney out of the boy.

The home we stayed in belonged to my granny, and the house was called *Ibrox*, much to the annoyance of my Dad, who was a huge Dons fan. Back in the '70s many folks had their granny at home, and she was a huge part of my early years. The fact that she owned the house and the name was *Ibrox* was a major influence in my brothers and I all following Glasgow Rangers FC.

Moving to Orkney was a brave decision, especially for Dad. My Mum was a born and bred Orcadian, she had moved to Aberdeen with her folks in the early '60s, so I do take my hat off to my Dad for making the brave move North to her island

WILL YOUR ANCHOR HOLD

Dad was a qualified carpenter(joiner) and could turn his hands to most things. He was practically gifted, but also a very good businessman, and, more importantly, he was a hard worker. Mum had been a lorry driver in Aberdeen, meaning both parents had no fear in doing something different.

In Orkney they were brave and opened a draper shop in the capital Kirkwall, which was fifteen miles from Stromness. The shop was named A&S Bain, the Levi shop, this shop was certainly a huge success and my parents would work in this shop for nearly twelve years.

Stromness is a beautiful town, with a population of roughly two thousand people, an amazing place to have spent my childhood, there was always lots happening, and I loved the town.

Life at home was eventful, my parents were often arguing, and this made home life uncomfortable - the smile I usually had on my face hid the heartache I felt. Granny would stay in the living room and dad in the kitchen, they did not talk, so as you can imagine this was an uncomfortable environment for all the family.

With dad and mum working all week, my granny was the major influence in the early days. She was a wonderful lady, always well-presented and her makeup was perfection in every way, her bright red lipstick was her trademark. From nursery to first year at the Academy, granny was my cornerstone and influence in my life, she was always available, and her tender nature was a stabiliser to me and my brothers. My oldest brother had an amazing relationship with her, he was very good to her.

The normal day back then would look like dad and mum leaving to go to Kirkwall, granny getting the freedom of the whole house to make breakfast for her boys. Coming home from school granny was always there, and we were well catered for, what a wonderful start in life.

I don't remember too much from nursery, but primary school was a blast from p1 to p7, fantastic memories of a wonderful school experience.

Primary school was a vibrant place, I loved it - great friends, good teachers and I did well at primary in the academic format. I've no idea what happened to me in the Academy, that will come later.

Football was always played at break and lunch times, this was brilliant for a boy who lived and breathed the beautiful game, in fact all the family were huge football fans. When the school bell rang out for the break or lunch time, we would sprint to the concrete pitch at the front of the primary school to play the beautiful game.

They say in life that we all gravitate to something we are good at, well with my grandad on my mum's side being one of the greatest players to grace the game in Orkney and also my mum being a talented

WILL YOUR ANCHOR HOLD

sports woman, the gift was passed on to me. Being small and having quick feet, my whole self would explode into life on the pitch, and this would be the case for many years to come.

Even in primary four I would be on the pitch with the older boys, which, back in the day, was brutal. With no referee and playing on concrete, it was not a good situation. The primary pitch had been grass, but several parents had complained about the messy trousers from the grass, so the school decided on a concrete pitch. Going from just dirty grass stained trousers to split knees was not the best result. This was a time long before the safety/risk assessments we now see everywhere. Actually playing with the older boys was a bonus, it made me play with wisdom and skill, keeping clear of the crazy tackles.

Primary school life was good, I enjoyed going to school, and the highlights were friends and football - I always had a smile on my face in this environment. Stromness Primary school was located in a fantastic spot overlooking the harbour and you could see way out to sea. Many a day I passed daydreaming from the school classroom windows.

Growing up, the football journey was my dream, like many a young boy, to be a professional player was the ultimate goal. However, something that may surprise many people, was my love of dancing. If I had the chance I would have loved to have learned tap dancing, yes you hear me, tap dancing.

WILL YOUR ANCHOR HOLD

This was not the thing to be sharing back in 1970s Orkney, can you imagine…. Ricky Bain doing tap dancing, "what a poofter!" would have been the shout.

I did perform in a couple of the school plays, one role was a Medieval Joker, which went down very well, and I enjoyed this role. Those that are close to me would say 'no surprise there' playing that role.

In another play I was given the role because of my big mouth, the character was a female ventriloquist dummy, called Jemima. The boy that was picked to play the part could not get the right voice, so I opened my mouth to imitate the voice and was given the role by the teacher. I was a bit embarrassed at the time, but looking back I loved every minute.

Going back to my granny, it was about p4 or p5 when I started to go to the Boys Brigade, she really encouraged me to go along. It was at this time that she gave me my first Bible, the first seeds of faith being planted.

In primary school there was always a visit from the church minister, he was a lovely gentle man, full of life and passion, and a great storyteller. He was there with his guitar and I embraced all the golden oldies, such as "He's got the whole world in his hands", "Give me oil in my lamp", "Father Abraham had many sons" and my favourite at the

WILL YOUR ANCHOR HOLD

time "I'm in the Lord's army", I loved doing the actions to this.

These were absolutely fantastic days, looking back, what an amazing time at the Stromness Primary School…. from enjoying the school work, obviously the sport and especially the football, as well as the school plays. There was Christian input at a young age, even then my heart was stirred and my spirit in me knew the voice of Jesus.

As you can tell from this opening chapter, football/ sport has been a huge factor and influence on my life, and from a young age, this was an area I excelled in.

I remember running to Primary School every day when the weather permitted, we stayed roughly half a mile from the school, no wonder I was fit back then. If I had asked my parents for a lift, the look my dad gave would have given the obvious answer, oh how times have changed!

The friends at school were great, and I'm still friends to this day with many of them, we were all blessed to have been brought up in such a beautiful place, and a time where health and safety didn't rule the world. To this day, my best friend is still living on the island, we became friends at nursery, and journeyed through the primary/ academy schools, maybe losing the closeness at the academy, but life brought us back together, and to this day we are very close.

WILL YOUR ANCHOR HOLD

Our time off from the primary, the weekends and long summer evenings, we were spoilt for choice, boredom was a swear word. We had so much to do, Stromness and the surrounding areas were our oyster, wow there was much to do and explore. From playing football, cycling, skateboarding, fishing of the piers, or under the pier (which looking back, was madness), Boys Brigade, Youth Club. Our lives were good, wholesome and extremely busy.

The late 70s early 80s, those were the days… the music, clothes, I am sounding old now, and we do tend to remember all the good things. You get the feel for my early years, life certainly was not mundane, the place, the era was a match for my character and personality, and I was never home, every opportunity I was outside exploring or, like most young boys, getting into trouble without knowing it.

Even from a young age I knew I had a different spirit, one that often got me in trouble or usually caused me to be misunderstood. God had a calling on my life from the day I was born, but at such a young age I had did not have a clue as to what lay ahead or what I would go through before it started to make sense.

Reaching Primary 7, I was doing not too badly in the academic field, as I shared earlier this would decrease in the academy. Sport was my area of

WILL YOUR ANCHOR HOLD

strength and confidence, and I was absolutely over the moon to have been made House Captain of Claymore, the inter-house at the school. The inter-house names were Claymore and Piper, named after oilfields in the North Sea (the Oil Industry was booming in the late 70s and early 80s). Flotta Oil Terminal was in full flow, with many Orkney locals making a great living from the oil industry. Like any young person, I was so excited to run home and tell my parents and granny that I had been made House Captain. Everyone was pleased for me and being made Captain was such an honour and responsibility too, I had to lead by example and try and stay out of trouble.

My other good friend in the primary was made Captain of Piper, so we became sporting rivals, but in the classroom a right pair of jokers and probably not a good combination. We had both been given many warnings by our teacher, and after yet another misdemeanour she finally lost the plot and we were both sent to the Headmaster, this was never good.

Our Headmaster was actually a really nice man, and had a gentle way about him, but once you crossed him we would see another side that no child wanted to be on the receiving end. The Headmaster, let`s just say was not in the mood for my friend and I, he tore the strips off us, and nearly tore the Captains badges off us too, we were both shocked and scared at the same time. A lesson learned, that's for sure. We were both on our best behaviour for the rest of

WILL YOUR ANCHOR HOLD

that week, and I would say we both performed really well as house Captains for the rest of P7.

From p1 right through to p7, primary school was a wonderful experience, and like I have shared, the memories will stay with me for the rest of my days. There are countless stories that I could share on this first chapter, but will finish off at the Stromness swimming pool….

Stromness has always been blessed on having brilliant sporting facilities, from the wonderful golf course, bowling green at the Point of Ness, to the magnificent football pitch at the Market Green at the North End of Stromness, the pitch where I have the most amazing memories. Just above the Market Green football pitch is the Stromness swimming pool, a place where I and so many kids had good fun in the water.

Probably around the age of eight years old, I found myself in the deep end, doggy paddle or just trying to stay afloat, the swimming coach appeared at the side of the pool "Mr Bain, can you swim a full length ?!". "Not sure but will give it ago" was my reply. I did the full length, not sure what kind of stroke, but I managed. The swimming coach asked if I would like to come along to the swimming club, so I said "YES".

My other friend was a really good swimmer, his sister was an amazing swimmer, probably the best female swimmer in Orkney. My swimming journey

WILL YOUR ANCHOR HOLD

was not too bad, but I could not manage to beat my friend, much to my frustration, he always got the gold medal, I was a silver or a bronze.

One night at swimming training the coach shouted that we get out the pool, he opened the fire exit door, it was wintertime and there was snow on the ground. We had to roll in the snow, then dive back into the pool. Imagine doing that now, or even a swimming coach asking a child to roll about in the snow! You know what, looking back it was not that bad, the pool felt warm after the snow experience.

I look back on this experience and also my football coach back in the '80s, a time where we were often pushed way beyond ourselves. At the time they felt unfair and often pushed us to breaking point, but now looking back, they made me into the character I am today, able to take the knocks that come our way in the battle of life.

There is way more I could write to finish off this first chapter, but hopefully I can fill in much more about the boy from Stromness as you journey with me in this book.

Before I go onto chapter two, a brief summary of chapter one, this boy from Stromness will always have fond memories of his childhood…

As you can see, my first love in sport is football, and you will see this theme throughout the book. The house I grew up in was called *Ibrox*, my

WILL YOUR ANCHOR HOLD

Granny was a massive Rangers supporter and my two brothers and I followed her in supporting the Gers- 'follow, follow' as they say.

The music taste back then was Elvis Presley, my best friend and I were both Presley fans, and blue noses, a good match we were, and still are to this day. The 70s & 80s were an amazing era, and the beautiful island of Orkney had a huge influence on my early years development, and in becoming the man I am today.

You can take the boy out of the island, but you cannot take the island out of the boy.

WILL YOUR ANCHOR HOLD

CHAPTER 2- RUNNING EVERYWHERE

I was so blessed to grow up in such a beautiful town, with the freedom to explore and really go wherever I wanted to go. My Parents would say "now be good and be home by 9pm or when it starts to get dark". As you can imagine, this boy made sure I would embrace, enjoy and get every ounce of the freedom that was readily available to the young people in Orkney.

The long summer months are still banked away in my memories, the long days and often 24 hours of light in Orkney, yes, a magical time!

If Forrest Gump was around then I reckon I would have given him a run for his money on the running front, I had one speed and that was flat out, full steam ahead.

We stayed on what was called the back road in Stromness, our home set high up over the town. We had amazing views from the large windows at the front of the house over the town and Scapa Flow, and from the West side of the house were the magnificent Hoy hills. Being a youngster I did not appreciate those wonderful scenic views.

Let`s go for the many positives and fun times in the Bain household, we were a close family, apart from my dad and granny who just did not get on with one another. Granny was a lovely lady with a heart of gold, a gentle lady who was a huge influence in my early days, she was always at home for all of us, with a listening ear and would share much wisdom with me.

She was a beautiful woman, always well-presented and had bright red lipstick, with often a cigarette, she actually made smoking look classy…….

To all the wider family (cousins etc), she was known as Mama, what a great name for a granny, so this is what I will call her going forward in the book.

Mama, as I shared, was the cornerstone to my brothers and I, dad and mum were through in Kirkwall six days a week running the Levi shop they owned in Kirkwall, the capital of Orkney.

Before going to school Mama was last person I saw and was the first person I met after school, she was home for her three grandsons, hence her influence of Glasgow Rangers was passed on. My Dad and Mum who were also both avid football fans, they were both Aberdeen supporters. So you can imagine the atmosphere on match day between Rangers and Aberdeen, unfortunately for the blue noses it was Aberdeen who had the upper hand in those days.

Mama`s late husband had died when I was only six months old in 1969, so I have no recollection of him. I still feel a bit cheated, since so much love and security comes from grandparents. He was known

WILL YOUR ANCHOR HOLD

as Dada to all the family, Mama and Dada it was, classy names for Grandparents.

Mama would often share about her husband, he had been a shrewd businessman and done well on the career front, but as a young boy it was his football stories and old photos that stirred this young boy's heart. Dada's football nickname was Yoka, due to the fact that he always had a raw egg before playing a match - this name was given to him and it stuck throughout his footballing career. He was the youngest player to score a hat-trick against Shetland, (Orkney's biggest rival). He also had the chance to go professional, but, unlike todays huge football wages, back in the 20's and 30's there was not the same superstar salaries. Dada had a good career, and this was his path, he did very well in the career department.

I loved it when it was only me and Mama in the living room at night because I had her undivided attention, and her story telling was first class. She was the one who gave me first Bible and encouraged me in looking to God. She influenced my Boys Brigade journey too, so the theme of my Christian walk was activated by Mama, I did not realise it back then, but looking back I see her hand upon my life of faith, the seed was planted, thank you Mama.

In the living room at *Ibrox*, Mama's seat was in the corner, this was her chair and we would only sit on

WILL YOUR ANCHOR HOLD

her throne if she was not in the room. The room was always in pristine condition, she loved a clean home. Beside her chair was the Rangers calendar for the year, she always had a calendar on the wall. On top of the sideboard behind her chair was a signed photo of her favourite Rangers player – Derek Parlane, a brilliant forward in the late 70`s, yes she was football crazy, which she passed onto her grandsons.

Elvis Presley was another love of her life, again this was passed onto me. I loved his music, his charisma and even the movies that were on during the school holidays, but I have to admit, most of these movies were very cheesy… even Elvis himself did not enjoy the roles he was given, apart from *Jail House Rock* and *King Creole*, which are still an excellent watch, the other movies can stay in the archives.

You are now getting a taste of my early years, and my relationship with Mama was a good one, she was a remarkable lady. My oldest brother, who is ten years older than me, had an amazing relationship with Mama. They were so good for one another, he knew how to treat her, and looking back he will still cherish those special memories.

My brothers and I shared a bedroom, three boys in one room, Dad had built a big extension to the house, he extended the kitchen and gave us boys a large bedroom to share. Looking back, there was not

WILL YOUR ANCHOR HOLD

any issues sharing the bedroom, we didn't know anything else, and my memories are good ones.

Going back to the start of this chapter, yes, the running everywhere, that was me - running to school, and certainly running home from school, probably even faster on the way home, the distance was roughly a 1/2 of a mile, not a bad run. Running was just so natural to me and it energised me, I came alive when the legs were working overtime, obviously a huge adrenaline rush, and with youth on my side too.

In the 70`s there was a popular TV series called the six-million-dollar man, here is the description of the series : Steve Austin is an astronaut who is seriously injured when his spaceship crashes. Handsome and athletic, Austin undergoes a government-sanctioned surgery, which rebuilds several of Steve`s body parts with machine parts, making him cyborg-like. When Steve recovers, his machine parts enable him to have superhuman strength and speed, as well as other powers. With these powers, Steve goes to work for the Office of Scientific Information, battling evil for the good of mankind.

Wow, what a hero this Steve Austin was, how could any young boy back in the 70`s not love this character? As you can imagine, I, like millions of other youngsters, made sure that we watched every episode of the six-million-dollar man. If we had SKY TV back in the day, then the six-million-dollar

WILL YOUR ANCHOR HOLD

man would have definitely been on 'series record', no doubt about this.

Today we have the Marvel movies, but back in the 70's there was only one, Steve Austin was the hero. Like any young boy does, we dream and want to copy the hero, so when running I thought I was going sixty mph, that was my reality as an eight year boy anyway. If you have seen the series, then you will know that Steve Austin's powers were his right arm, both legs and left eye are replaced with "bionic" implants that enhance his strength , speed and vision far above human norms: he can run at speeds of over sixty mph, and his eye has a 20:1 zoom lens and infrared capabilities, while his bionic limbs all have the equivalent power of a bulldozer.

Yes, we did try the impossible to match our hero, like jumping off high walls and doing other stupid things that our little bodies were not designed to do. There were many injuries for the young ones trying to match the six-million-dollar man. The hospital A&E departments were overrun by young boys with broken arms, ankles etc, proving that we all look for a hero.

Going back to the description of Steve Austin, he was battling evil for the good of mankind, sounds like the person who did battle evil to save all of mankind, I will introduce him to you later in the book.

WILL YOUR ANCHOR HOLD

They say that gifts are passed down through the family line, music is a gift, singing is gift and yes sport is a gift, it's all in the genes, and I fully agree on this matter. My Mum was very sporty in her youth, from playing hockey and badminton, as well as a fast runner. In fact I was told she used to play football with the lads, unfortunately back then the girl's football was a no-go. Thank goodness times have changed and the girls football is on the up.

Dad was a very good runner; he did say he played football but not too sure about that. He was musical though, a talented saxophone player, he loved to relax playing the sax.

So, the running genes were passed down to me and my second oldest brother, he was even quicker than me, unfortunately my oldest brother was not so quick, sorry brother if you are reading this. My oldest brother had asthma, this put a hold on his sport. Thankfully he seemed to grow out of the asthma, and this no longer bothers him.

At school of course I loved and embraced PE, this certainly was my favourite and most productive class in the primary. I know PE is like marmite to kids, for those who loved sport it was fantastic, but for those who were not sporty then these classes would have felt like torture and not enjoyable. Let's be honest, we all love doing things we are good at, and dread doing things that we cannot do very well.

WILL YOUR ANCHOR HOLD

Academically I am in the 'very average' category, yet back in primary school I was on the higher scale. It's strange what happened, but my I will write about this later in the book.

Let's go back to running - as I have shared, when running it was like I was born to do this, my soul would leap with joy running everywhere, free as a bird, no worries, no issues, just my legs going full pelt. Sports day at primary school was the day my heart would pump quicker and the butterflies in the tummy were churning away, excitement was in the air.

Primary 1 and 2 I was in third place in the flat sprint, from P3 onwards I came first in the sprint. P7 was eventful, I was not the fastest person in the class, there was a girl who could beat all the boys, she was a flying machine.

I remember the boys race for P7 like it was yesterday, I got off to a flying start and felt I was winning comfortably, then nearing the finishing line someone was very close. I had to dip at the line, yes I won, but the boy who was right beside me on the finishing line was someone who came out of nowhere, we didn't even know that he could run, what a surprise, from that moment I learned to write off no-one.

As I said, I dipped at the finish line, the competitive spirit in me did not like to lose, was I bad loser? I

WILL YOUR ANCHOR HOLD

didn't think so, but I'm sure my friends will say different.

Sport was huge in my life in the Primary, and still is, and growing up in Stromness was brilliant for any sportsperson - there was an 18 hole golf course, bowling green, tennis courts, swimming pool, badminton, squash court, sailing, and of course the big football pitch called the Market Green.

The Market Green was like my theatre of dreams, the place where I could be myself and do what I loved - playing football, running was fantastic, but to do it with a ball, well these two went well together, like I was born to dribble, running at pace, changing direction, yep that was me. When the men were playing at the Market Green, they always got a good crowd, the locals from Stromness were great at supporting the local football team. The season in Orkney runs from April to September, so light nights and weather in general pretty good, at least that's what I like to remember.

My friends, and many other of the lads from Stromness, would have our own game on the training pitch beside the Market Green, eyes half on the mens game and playing teams on our pitch. We would play all night if allowed, or until exhausted, at that age it was like we were all running on Duracell batteries, our stamina levels were pretty impressive. Where we lived certainly benefited our fitness, we would either be running to the Market

WILL YOUR ANCHOR HOLD

Green or racing on the bikes, a great combination for fitness.

Stromness for a youngster was a magical place, and with the vast open spaces, we could venture anywhere, this was certainly a massive benefit for a healthy lifestyle. We either walked, ran or cycled all over the town and outer town, so if we had Strava back in those days then our steps count for a day would have been through the roof, well over 20,000 steps probably.

Stromness means "Headland protruding into the tidal system". In Viking times, the anchorage where Stromness now stands was called *Hamnavoe*, meaning "peaceful" or "safe" harbour.

For my parents, Stromness was indeed a safe harbour for their boys and all the parents will have felt the same way. Stromness was a place where the kids were encouraged and given permission to go and explore, what an amazing place, and still is. There is a saying "you don't realise what you have until it is gone", this is so true.

My early years in life were spent mainly running, cycling, climbing and doing things that my parents would be shaking their head at now. With being at Youth club, Boys Brigade, swimming and football training my life was full on and I loved every minute.

WILL YOUR ANCHOR HOLD

Looking back, the highlights in the early years were winning my first football medal with the Boys Brigade in 1978, I was nine years old and played a part in the winning goal when I was tripped in the box, and it was a penalty. There was no diving in those days, it was drilled into us to stay on your feet, unlike today's game.

The guy who is still a huge influence in my life was my Boy's Brigade Captain at the time, and he was in charge of the football team that day. That same weekend I was staying in a place called Birsay, I was there with the Stromness Youth Club, a weekend away, and the football tournament was the same weekend. Thanks to my BB Captain, I was able to go to both. After winning the Final, which was 2-1 against the Finstown BB's, I was so excited to be driven to Birsay to show off the shield.

Football was always first choice in sport, and this was evident when the swimming coach said to me "Ricky, you know that there has to be a choice between swimming and football if want to go to higher level with the swimming". Well there was only one winner in this, and football it was.

In the swimming, I was an ok swimmer, and probably would have improved with upping the training schedule, but football came naturally to me and I knew that by focusing on this sport, I would be very decent on the football pitch.

WILL YOUR ANCHOR HOLD

With the Youth Club football I travelled South a few times, having won the Orkney Youth Club tournament, the winners were invited to the Scottish event. This involved teams from all over Scotland, which was a real honour and wonderful achievement. The only downside was the distance that the Orkney contingent had to travel, and I was a terrible traveller in my younger days, you name it - car, bus, boat sickness, that was me. The biggest battle I had was the thought of having to travel, I absolutely hated the boat, sea sickness is horrible. Imagine, catching the early boat from Orkney to Thurso, then a bus to the Central belt, usually Edinburgh, this was a nightmare for anyone who had travel sickness.

We did this journey three times in my Youth Club days, we never won the tournament, but gave a very good account of ourselves. After a game, a scout from Stirling Albion FC came up to me and said I had all the attributes to go far in the game, he said he would watch out for me in the years ahead. The big downside back then was obviously staying miles away from the Central Belt and not much chance of progression staying on an island off the North of Scotland. Thankfully there seems to be more of a chance for the Orkney lads to go to a higher level these days.

The title for this chapter is *Running Everywhere*, I am glad I chose this title, since while writing this chapter many memories have come flooding back,

WILL YOUR ANCHOR HOLD

and those memories that have been hidden away have emerged from the old grey matter.

The film Forrest Gump sees a young boy with a gift to run and run, full pelt all the way, a brilliant movie if you have never watched it. I was certainly not Forrest, but, like the movie, the freedom and energy I felt running was unbelievable, it was like I was designed to do it, and this will be an important thread throughout my story.

In the book of Hebrews, chapter 12, verses 1-3

Therefore, since we are surrounded by such a great cloud of witnesses, let us throw off everything that hinders and the sin that so easily entangles. And let us run with perseverance the race marked out for us, fixing our eyes on Jesus, the pioneer and perfecter of faith. For the joy set before him he endured the cross, scorning its shame, and sat down at the right hand of the throne of God. Consider him who endured such opposition from sinners, so that you will not grow weary and lose heart.

That is what I did as a youth, I threw off everything that hinders, I just went for it full steam ahead, one hundred mph, in my race. Life was the race, but, unlike the scripture above, my eyes were not fixed on Jesus, I was more often running head first into trouble without the guidance of faith.

Faith will come up a lot in this book, and you will hear about the transformation in my life, but the

WILL YOUR ANCHOR HOLD

battle has been a fierce one, you are going to experience my mountain top wins and also the dark valley experiences that I have encountered.

Please keep reading as I take you on this life journey...

WILL YOUR ANCHOR HOLD

CHAPTER 3 – BEHIND THE SMILE

There is not a family on this planet that is perfect. Even though we all know that so well, in today's modern culture we put on the front or maybe the mask. Not the Covid one, but the mask that all is well, life is good. Social media is full of the happy families, all is great, and the sun is shining. It's better to put on a smile that have a crying face, yes, I agree 100%.

In my world the big smile was actually my coping mechanism and I became very good at having the happy persona, where most would have thought Ricky has it all. Our family had no money worries, both Mum and Dad working together in a successful business, it all looked stable and successful in the eyes of the world.

The Levi shop which my parents owned was an awesome business venture, my Dad took a loan to open the Levi shop, and the rest, as you say, is history. They made a good living from this shop, and Levi jeans or clothes in general was the gear to wear in the late 70s and early 80s. At that time in Orkney, A&S Bain was the only Levi outlet was in Orkney. The location of the shop in Bridge Street, Kirkwall was the near perfect location as well, plenty of footfall in the capital of Orkney. Mum and Dad were both hard working and gave their all to family and business. Mum had the people skills and

WILL YOUR ANCHOR HOLD

my dad the business acumen, a great combination for a successful Levi shop.

Mum was an Orcadian born and bred, and she loved the island lifestyle. Obviously with being born and bred she had grown up to embrace the Orkney life. She was kind, extremely likeable, lovely-natured and heart of gold, a fantastic Mum to all her boys.

I was born in Aberdeen in 1969, and moved to Orkney 1970. My oldest brother had attended school in Aberdeen, but was now in school in Stromness, my middle brother was three years older, just about ready for primary school.

Mum had a massive stroke in 1970, she was fortunate to survive; the story is that she was due to be playing badminton and did not feel too good so gave badminton a miss. Knowing mum she must have felt bad because she loved her sport and did not want to miss out. Mum woke dad up in the middle of the night to say she could not move her left side, so an emergency airlift to Aberdeen began the long recovery. She had to learn how to talk and walk again, and she never did fully recover, always walking with a slight limp and her speech was slurred.

Dad…. well, they say opposites attract, and he was certainly the opposite of mum - he was impatient, quick tempered, always in a hurry and maybe not a people person. He was, however, a good dad, hardworking and always willing to help those in need, though most folks did not see this side of him. He was Aberdonian, a man from the North East of Scotland. Looking back on his life, he came from a hard-working family. Growing up on a croft with his parents and four siblings, they did not have much, and hard work was their way out. His father and that older generation were of a harder breed than those of us today, and my dad carried this often-harder exterior for the most of his days. I only actually saw this softening in his later years.

Our family dynamic was difficult, with granny owning the home and staying in the living room if dad was at home, due to the fact they did not see eye to eye. This made life very difficult for mum and, as you can imagine, the atmosphere in the home was deeply affected by this 'non relationship'.

I did share earlier that my oldest brother had an amazing relationship with granny, he was very good to her, and it was lovely to see such a close bond. Dad was harder on my oldest brother than me and middle brother. Maybe most parents are harder on the oldest child, something I will never know due to being the baby of the family.

My middle brother was born in 1966, unfortunately during delivery there was severe lack of oxygen to his brain. Oxygen deprivation at birth is linked to a number of conditions that include cerebral palsy, and epilepsy. These babies can suffer from cognitive problems, intellectual deficiencies and

WILL YOUR ANCHOR HOLD

developmental delays as they grow older, compared to babies who do not suffer from such oxygen deprivation. So basically my middle brother had the mental age of an eight-year-old, and this was tough on mum and dad too, back then there was not the same help or understanding of what my brother and parents had to face going forward.

Yep, no family is perfect, and most have challenges to face that no one knows about, the dynamics in a family do shape the lives of those growing up in the culture. Many a time coming home in the evenings was like walking into a battle ground; raised voices, swearing and just a horrible place to come home too. It was my dad doing the shouting, going off on one, and boy when he lost his temper it was time to scamper! At the time as a young boy it was scary and heart-breaking seeing the two people who I loved the most at war with one another.

Home should be a safe place, a sanctuary for any child - it was when dad was not at home, but when he was home, the family atmosphere was one of tender hooks, waiting for him to explode. I am not slating my dad, just being transparent, open and honest, no stone unturned. Like most young boys fathers, he was, and still is, a hero to me. His own journey in life was a hard road and he did not know (or was not shown) how to express himself emotionally in a healthy way.

WILL YOUR ANCHOR HOLD

My safe place was the outside world, and Stromness was my safe haven, and that is why most of my childhood was outside, or even going to a friend`s house. My best friend`s home was a welcoming home and I would often be there, they always made me feel welcome and I will be forever thankful to this family, wonderful folks with hearts of gold. If I couldn`t find anyone to play with or hang about with, then I would walk the streets of Stromness on my own or along the beach, even in the wind and rain, just to get away from home if my parents were arguing.

I made sure if I met people then my big cheesy grin would appear and sure everyone thought, what a happy young man. Many would say "No wonder he`s happy, his folks are loaded, and he gets free Levi clothes". Unfortunately, nothing has changed in society, we all look at what people have - status, money etc. It's all what the eye sees, the world looks at the external image, the superficial front.

Looking back, I was treated differently because of my folks owning a business. To those on the outside I came from a good family line, Mama and Dada had been business owners too, so owning a business meant having money and being a success.

My persona was one of confidence and I believe my natural being is one of happiness, even back then I was secure in my own skin and had good discernment in reading those around me. However

WILL YOUR ANCHOR HOLD

my home was a powder keg, and most nights heading home I would wonder if there was argument in the mix when I opened the front door. On a fine summer night, if there was no wind, and I was heading home after a day out with my friends, I could hear my Dad shouting the closer I got to home. I'm sure other people would have heard the shouting too. If dad was going off on one, then I would often walk past the house and walk around the town again.

Basically, I got used to this way of life, and learned to accept that this was what me and my brothers would have to live with, those were some difficult times when you look back.

To me, dad had a good life, he had an active life and was involved with the golf, bowls and in the winter played in the Darts league. At home he was gifted with being a qualified joiner, so, as I have shared, he built the extended kitchen and our bedroom onto the house. He was a hardworking man and would always be doing something to add value to the home and make life better for his family.

Our childhoods are vital in moulding us into the adults that we will become, so I know for my Dad, that his upbringing played a massive factor in who he became. Men still find it hard to talk about their emotions and how they feel, but thankfully there is help these days and more men are opening up, talking about their emotions.

WILL YOUR ANCHOR HOLD

Well, back in the late 70s, early 80s 'men were men' as they say, and my dad never spoke about his feelings, emotions and, more importantly, his frustrations in life. They say that when men get fearful then anger will come to the surface, and when dad felt fear for his family or maybe the business and all the other stresses of life, he did not have anyone to go too to express how he felt and this meant he would lose his temper quickly, letting rip. Those closest to him were the target of his temper, and this meant we often lived in fear.

Like I said, from the outside, we had a beautiful house, successful work life, but behind the scenes there was always a volcano about to erupt and this created an uneasy atmosphere in the home, which should have been a safe sanctuary for any family. If dad was in a good mood, then he was brilliant fun, and would chase us around house, and his laugh was contagious, he had a fantastic sense of humour, That is what I want to remember him for, and I have forgiven him, in my heart and memories he is still my hero. Like I shared, my story is transparent, and I will write what I have experienced, the whole truth.

Running or playing sport, especially playing football, was my escape from everything, and my parents were a huge support, they were always there for the evening games I played. Mum praising my game and dad advising that I could do better. On the pitch I felt safe, it was my safe place, and football came naturally to me, with being quick and good balance, my DNA was designed for the beautiful game. The smile on my face was beaming on the field, especially if we won. Yes I loved to win, my competitive edge was evident from a young age, and it`s still there, I just try and manage it more maturely these days.

Smiling helps reduce stress-induced hormones in the bloodstream, which helps avoid adrenal fatigue. Smiling enhances positive and negative emotions swimming around your mind. When you choose to smile and laugh often, you tap into your positive emotions.

Yes, smiling was my coping mechanism, thankfully my attitude was, and is still, positive. Don't get me wrong, my thought life can go negative, but my battle is to quickly go back to the positive mindset. Confidence in who you are is one thing, and having a wee swagger plus a smile can irk people, so often I would often hear "Bain, you are a cocky peedie so and so". *Peedie* in Orcadian means little/small, so not being too tall, I often heard these comments, or sometimes worse! Looking back, I was a bit cocky, but can truly say that I did not have a bad bone in my body or had any ill feeling towards anyone.

Thankfully I did not really experience being bullied, I know a few guys did not like me, so I usually kept out of their way. One night at Youth Club a guy grabbed a hold of my shirt and gave me a full-on

WILL YOUR ANCHOR HOLD

Glasgow kiss, right on the bridge of nose. I did literally see stars, and my nose was in agony. Looking back I was in shock too, because I had nothing against this guy, but he obviously had something against me. The smile was gone, replaced with pain and the tears began to flow. Why would someone do this for no good reason? The guy who did it, said "It`s because you are a peedie cocky f..ker and needed the smile wiped off your face". Thankfully a couple of the older lads dragged him away and told him to "F..k off".

My dad was furious when he saw the mess of my face, and he was going to go after the guy, but once dad calmed down and under much persuasion from mum, he decided to let it go. Dad was protective of his family, and this was always the case growing up, he had my back if I was the innocent party. If not, then he would call it out and made sure that I did not fall fowl or do something stupid, then there would be consequences for my actions.

The guy who did headbutt me was an angry individual, yet he did not bother me physically again, verbally yes, but never in a physical way. There were one or two who did give me a smack, or bend my arm up my back, but that was it growing up - no more bullying, thank the Lord.

Being secure in myself, even with living in an often-volatile atmosphere at home, my natural default was to smile. I enjoyed walking around Stromness with

WILL YOUR ANCHOR HOLD

the attitude of, if I smile at someone then you receive the same back, and for the majority of people, this was true. As you know though, there is always one who has the grumpy persona no matter how big a smile you give.

My early years growing up in Stromness, were full on, plenty to do for a young boy who loved the action : Youth Club, Boys Brigade, Football and much more, was like heaven for me, I absolutely embraced the island upbringing.

I want to finish this chapter by honouring my Granny/Mama, a grandparent is a huge influence on a child, and Mama was a wonderful lady, a huge influence on me. She was the lady who named her house *Ibrox*, hence me and my two brothers following Rangers, much to the disappointment of my Dad. Mama was a steady presence in the home, in fact she was there all the time, apart from a day in Kirkwall to go shopping. Early morning or late at night Mama was available, the happy go-to.

I remember the last time I saw her too, it was 1981 and I came home from school with my Auntie in a panic. She had come around to visit Mama, and unusually the door was locked. Back then hardly anyone locked the front door, yet for some reason Mama had locked the door.

Mama had fallen in her bedroom and could not move; we could see her through the bedroom window. With me being so wee and nimble, I was

WILL YOUR ANCHOR HOLD

able to squeeze through my bedroom window and unlock the front door. My Auntie called the ambulance, and Mama was taken to Balfour Hospital, where they said that she had broken her hip. Mama never made it home again, she took ill with pneumonia in hospital and passed away.

I still remember the phone call late at night, my dad took the call, and mum knew by his voice on the phone and ran through to the kitchen in tears. Both mum and dad smoked, so that was their first go to, light a cigarette and digest the bad news. I was twelve years old when Mama died, there would be a huge hole in all the family`s lives going forward. For me and my brothers, our steady influence in our lives was now gone, we were utterly heart broken. Mama was the person who made sure I joined the Boys Brigade, she gave my first Bible too, a beautiful leather bible, KJV – King James Version, a Bible I still have to this day.

My memories of Mama are tucked in my heart, all wonderful memories that will last a lifetime. She was a pillar in the family, an amazing granny, who left a legacy to all who knew her. The love that comes from a Granny is absolutely irreplaceable; they have the life skills, the experience, wisdom and the patience that only a well-lived life can give, something you cannot get from a book or second-hand information.

WILL YOUR ANCHOR HOLD

Mama, you were amazing, loving, wise, and you gave us your best. The only grandparent I had a relationship with, since Dada died when I was 6 months old, and my dad's parents stayed in Aberdeen and only saw them once a year at best.

Grandparents are a gift, you don't know what you have until it's gone, and that was certainly what happened with Mama. When she passed the pain was vast, and she left a huge void in my life. At the age of twelve, Mama's death was my first loss, and nothing will prepare you for it. They say time is a healer, but you never truly get over it, you simply learn to manage the loss.

WILL YOUR ANCHOR HOLD

CHAPTER 4 – FINDING MY IDENTITY

The teenage years are all about finding out who you are or "Who am I"? What is life all about?

This was me back in the 80s, at the age of thirteen years old and now in the Academy, life was becoming oh so different from the primary school years. Primary was a safe, comfortable environment for me. Now we enter the big school… Stromness Academy to a boy was a huge variety of various buildings sprawled out in the back road of Stromness.

With Stromness being the main town on the West side of Orkney, the Academy was the place all the academy-age pupils from all over the various villages in the West came too. Yep, exciting but also scary days were ahead for me, and the many others, starting 1st year.

Meeting new people did not faze me, and I soon made new friends. Of course, with human nature the way it is, not everyone can be called a friend. School Summer holidays are usually always wonderful memories for most children, and looking back, they did feel like long beautiful sunny days.

Going from P7 to 1st year is hard for any kid, you are going from the oldest (Top Dog) in the Primary to being the youngest, smallest in the big Academy. Sure, we all felt this experience as daunting and first day in the Academy has to be one where you are so

WILL YOUR ANCHOR HOLD

nervous. Every child needs a friend and your friendship group at this age was crucial, knowing you had friends who had your back and that you were not alone was a major comfort, even to a confident looking boy like me, I hid these doubts and emotions well.

There were children from all over the West mainland, I did know some of the lads from playing football against them in the Primary. But the majority were all new to one another, and the first few weeks of the Academy was finding your feet and getting to know one another. In first year, all those above did seem like giants, especially from 4th year upwards, so my attitude and mindset was keeping my head down and don't get involved in anything stupid.

Life was different now, before I left for school from home in the mornings, my parents and older brother had already left to go to Kirkwall for work. This is when I really missed Mama, she was the one who always had been there, the constant presence in my life, now gone but certainly not forgotten, she was the best.

I usually left the house for school with my middle brother, he enjoyed my company on the way to school, which looking back must have been hard for him with not fitting in due to his disability. Back in the early 80s there was not the same understanding or help for those who were different to the

WILL YOUR ANCHOR HOLD

mainstream population. My middle brother was amazing and because he had grown up in Stromness all the locals knew him, and the majority embraced who he was and made him feel secure.

As we know, there are those who can be cruel and mean, and yes, he was a target for them, and they were brutal. With me being just a 1st year and my middle brother in 4th year, I did get to witness and hear what others said about him. This did cause a couple of fights and verbal confrontations, I was deeply protective of him, and most of the fights I had were sticking up for him.

There was a particular guy at school, who was the school bully, and most of the school didn't go near him. One day we had a face to face at the back of the school, and I did say to him that he might win the fight, but he would be in one, that's for sure, I would not back down. Even then I could not stand a bully, and this guy was number one in the bully stakes. Thankfully he never did come near me, and we would make sure that we avoided one another in the school years. I know it says in the Bible to 'turn the other cheek', but for me there has to be time to stand up for yourself, or someone else.

The name-calling was severe for my middle brother and a certain word (spastic) was like red rag to a bull, yes kids can be cruel, that's for sure.

On one occasion Dad was summoned to school, what had happened was that my middle brother had

WILL YOUR ANCHOR HOLD

been bullied leading up to this day and finally took things into his own hands. He had put one of the guys who bullied him through a glass window of a door, he had unbelievable strength and these bullies had found that out the hard way.

The lead up to this fight was a long build up in name-calling and continuous pushing my brother around. One day my middle brother had come home upset and my Dad asked him what was wrong, after hearing my brother`s story Dad said "Well next time they lay a hand on you, just give them an uppercut on the chin", and my brother loved Dad, and was fully compliant to this instruction.

Dad had a good positive chat with the Headmaster, and the outcome was that the boys who had made my brother`s life at school unbearable were suspended for a while, and my brother was never really bothered again, well not to my knowledge anyway.

First year was exciting and so much going on, with new classes, new friends and new adventures to be had, and yes lots of nice-looking girls! As I shared from my Primary school days, academically the Primary had gone well, and in first year I was in the top class for maths, middle group for English and things were looking good going forward.

The school had four inter house names, *Magnus*, *Sigurd*, *Rognvald* and the house I was in *Thorfinn*. Magnus was named after Saint Magnus, Sigurd was

WILL YOUR ANCHOR HOLD

named after Earl Sigurd of Orkney, Rognvald, named after the Christian saint who came to Orkney, and finally Thorfinn, who was named after Earl Thorfinn of Orkney.

With me being the keen sportsman, I was delighted to have been voted to be the House Captain for Thorfinn, a role that I would do for the remainder of my school years, right through to 5th Year.

Sport, especially football, was my identity in my school years. I was indeed football daft, I lived and breathed this game, and as we all know, if you are good at something, then you want to do or perform this as much as possible. My physical being was made for the game, and I made sure that I would spend as much time as possible honing my whole being in improving myself to be the best.

Football was my go-to in life, whether playing or watching the game, I loved watching the live matches on TV, especially Glasgow Rangers. Unlike today, where there can be a live match nearly every night on the box, back in the early 80s, it was usually just a semi-final or Cup final day when a match would be shown live. Rangers were not the best team in the early 80s, they struggled through these years. Aberdeen were an amazing team, managed by Alex Ferguson, and they would beat Real Madrid in that famous final in Gothenberg in 1983. I still remember my dad dancing in the kitchen when John Hewitt scored the winning goal,

WILL YOUR ANCHOR HOLD

what an achievement for the Dons. There was a song called 'he's football crazy, he's football mad', and yes that was me along with a few of my friends, we were indeed football crazy.

So at school my identity was in the beautiful game, and I certainly played up to it, and have to admit that it consumed my everyday thoughts, not always a good thing for my academic progress.

With home life not the best, and weighing up what kind of humour my dad would come home with, played on mind, all the time. These were days when no one asked about mental health or wellbeing, you just had to get on with it and tuck away the issues. Putting on the big smile, when I was actually crying inside.

First and Second years at school were finding your feet in the Academy, finding the friendship groups and knowing what subjects that you were good at, or comfortable with. As I know with my own kids, the Academy years go past in a flash, and before you know it, it is time to move on into the big bad world.

Third year was the time to get your head down, study and apply myself more than I had done in the first two years. The parents evenings that my folks attended had the usual responses from the teachers : he has the potential to do well, but far too easily distracted and clowns around far too much.

WILL YOUR ANCHOR HOLD

The amount of homework had drastically increased, and this was the major problem for me. You see if the parents were arguing then I could not get my head down to study anything, and I just wanted to be outside, anywhere in fact, as long as I got away from the shouting. Dad could really shout and his language was shocking, with having worked in the building trade, his industrial language was well used within the four walls of our home. Again, I am not saying this to dishonour my dad, just saying it the way it was back then. No matter the weather, I made my excuses to leave the house, if it was summertime, then with the good weather and lighter nights, I was out till ten pm. There was always a place to go, I did find it easy to make friends and was comfortable in any company.

Ibrox (our home) was on situated high up on the back road of Stromness, and at the bottom of the road was a place called Faravel, which at the time was council houses. A place where I would have so much fun, laughter and enjoyment. But I did have to do it the hard way in the earlier years, with not being from Faravel, I had to persevere to get to know the kids from Faravel, and this was not easy looking back. I remember the first night I went down from my home and the kids were not too friendly, got into a fight and someone actually bit my bum, leaving teeth marks on my right bottom cheek, and there was blood too. Dad went off the head the head when he found out that someone had bitten my bum, he was for sorting them out. I can laugh now about this embarrassing story, but at the time it was far from funny.

Perseverance would become my middle name in life, and this is what I did with the kids at Faravel, I kept coming back and eventually made friends with this crazy gang. In the summer months, we would play kick the can, run along the top of the walls playing catch, absolutely off our heads looking back. Lighting fires was another favourite, and thankfully they never spread out of control. The Faravel folks were so down to earth and great fun to be around, my Auntie and Uncle also stayed at Faravel, so I would visit them often, and knew I would be well fed, or a drink of juice was to be had.

This of course did not help my schoolwork, with homework not getting done or doing as little as possible, my academic journey was now beginning to suffer. I dropped from the top group in Maths to bottom, my school learning was in freefall. I went about school like I didn't care, but deep inside I was hurting, feeling like a failure. Again, the big smile showed that to everyone looking on "Ricky is always smiling- he has it all together- what a lucky boy".

Between Faravel, going to Youth Club, Badminton, Boys Brigade and of course football, my life was hectic, so this gave me the chance to hide that feelings of failure. My identity back then was being

WILL YOUR ANCHOR HOLD

busy doing things, and as you can see by the above, it was an active lifestyle, you can throw in cycling and skateboarding to the above too.

Breaking it down, I was truly blessed in the amount of stuff that I did in the 80s, but my school work was suffering due to my home life, and I could have handled it better, but cannot go back in time.

My best friend in Primary had found another friendship group in the Academy, we kind of drifted apart, yet at the same time had each other`s back, always there for each other.

Youth Club was the place to be, and you would find me upstairs in the games hall with my friends playing football all night if we were allowed. This was the place where I honed my football skills, from keepie-ups to tight close control in the hall. I loved every minute of Youth Club, plus the adventures of going south with the football team, brilliant memories. On the nights at Youth Club, they were always action packed and most enjoyable, after Youth Club ended, my friends and I used to race to the chipper, there were 2 different ways in getting to the Chipper, and it was hilarious seeing the boys thinking they were running in the Olympic games to be first in the Chip shop, which looking back was an amazing chip shop, with of course with newspapers being the wrapping material back in the day. The Youth Club hall was one of my finest moments playing against Kirkwall Grammar School when I

WILL YOUR ANCHOR HOLD

was in 2nd year, playing 5 a side, inter school, we were trailing 2-6 at half-time, our PE teacher was going off his head. Well, we won the match 7-6, and I scored all five in the second half, a story I have told many times lol.

As you can see so far, my identity was football back then, the boy who smiled all the time, played football and wore the Levi gear, the Levi kid. To those on the outside "Ricky Bain has it all, good at sport, always a smile and gets all the latest Levi gear from his Parents", I heard this expression all the time. Yes, I hid it well, not wanting to disappoint my parents with telling the truth. In fact, I would make excuses to my friends if they wanted to come up to my house, in case my parents were shouting. I remember saying to one friend "I have big holes in the floors due to building work", which was a lie, he even goes on about it to this day. Little did he know that I was frightened to go back home, I was always more comfortable going to a friend`s home.

The Boys Brigade was the perfect way in ending the week, yes, we were back at school on a Friday evening, but it was my favourite place at school, in the gym hall. Now, this was the perfect hall for Boys Brigade, a good size gym hall, to play football, soft ball, basketball and of course the crash mat or medicine ball to play murder ball.

WILL YOUR ANCHOR HOLD

Murder ball was a game that with today's health and safety regulation would probably fail the average risk assessment. The medicine ball or crash mat up on its side in the middle of the hall, with two teams on opposite ends of the hall, the rules were simply to get the ball or crash mat to the end of the hall, like scoring a goal. There were no rules too, just full on young lads doing their upmost getting the ball or mat to the opposing end. As you can imagine chaos reigned, and there were injuries, but the officers did step in if things got out of control.

Boys Brigade was a safe place for many boys back in my youth, and with the various ages from 1st to 6th year in the Senior Boys Brigade section, this made for an interesting Boys Brigade journey, where you did have to stick up for yourself, yes there were and still are, those who are bullies. For me, I was able to stick up for myself both verbally and physically, and there were times I had to use both, since the beginning of time there had sadly been this silly culture on some older boys picking on those below them. I will share more about the Boys Brigade in the next chapter, there is much to share in this happy place for me.

As I draw to a close the chapter I have named 'Finding my Identity', what has been evident while writing this book is that a major influence in my early years growing up in Stromness was my Granny/Mama. She was my safe place and direction in the early years that develop a person as a

WILL YOUR ANCHOR HOLD

youngster, I do thank her and also thank God for giving me such a beautiful, caring person as a young boy.

I have not really covered my faith journey as yet. Mama was a huge influence in this area, she encouraged me to join the Boys Brigade and gave me first Bible when I was about 9 or 10 years old. I don't know if she prayed for me or if she had a deep faith, but she had what is called the Fruit of the Spirit : love, joy, peace, patience, kindness, generosity, faithfulness, gentleness, self-control. Those who are in Christ are distinguished from unbelievers in that they have been gifted with the Holy Spirit, enabling them to bear this kind of fruit (Galatians 5 v 22-23).

It's often said that many can talk the talk, Mama talked and walked it too, a woman who was a pillar in the community of Stromness as a young lady. She was the woman who gave me security, love and much wise guidance as a young boy. Mama loved all her grandchildren, my brothers and I were so fortunate to live in the same house as her, knowing she was available 24/7, with a kind word and a gentle smile to take away the worries of life back then.

To those of you who have a great relationship with your Grandparents, hold them tightly and treasure them. The children I have, all five of them, had a good relationship with Granda Sandy, until he

WILL YOUR ANCHOR HOLD

passed away. They have a wonderful relationship with Bampa and G-ma, and I know that my kids will look back one day and be so thankful for the amazing relationship they had with their truly awesome Grandparents.

Psalm 92 v 14 – *They will still bear fruit in old age; they will stay fresh and green.*

WILL YOUR ANCHOR HOLD

CHAPTER 5 – LIFE IS AN ADVENTURE

My teenage years were certainly carefree in that I could come and go when I pleased, and I had an awesome time in these days, apart from the atmosphere at home when my parents were arguing. If Dad was in a good mood, then all was well, but if he was in a bad mood then this would affect the whole household. Mum was level headed, much like her mother, she had a wonderful temperament, which was attractive to the many folks who knew her.

The greatest adventures that I had were with the Boys Brigade, especially the summer camps that we would go on. I went to Rackwick, which was on the island of Hoy, an absolutely beautiful location on a popular island in Orkney. The location of the famous Old Man of Hoy, a 449- foot sea stack. In 1750, the Old Man was depicted as a headland, but by the 1820`s stormy seas had carved the rock into a stack arch- two legs gave the Old Man his name. We also went to Dornoch in 1982, the reason I remember this date so vividly is because the World Cup was be played in Spain. The weather was amazing that year as well, we had beautiful sunshine for the ten days we were away in Dornoch.

The camp in Peebles was 1984 I think, another wonderful camp, and again the weather was remarkable, in fact probably too hot for the Orkney boys!

WILL YOUR ANCHOR HOLD

I'll write about the Rackwick camps first, think I went to two Boys Brigade camps to Rackwick, and looking back, both times the weather was very good….

These camps were full on and action packed, a dream for any young teenage boy, doing life with your mates and away from the parents, amazing. Nestled among the Hoy Hills is beautiful Rackwick Bay. This crofting township is considered one of the most beautiful places in Orkney. Bounded by towering 200m cliffs and steep heathery hills, Rackwick Valley rests beside a fine sand and boulder strewn beach. It has a beauty and climate all of its own. The walk to the Old Man of Hoy starts here. Rackwick is a good place for campers with a traditional bothy building open to the use of the public.

Around forty boys were at this camp, split into teams of nine to ten, we stayed in the old army style bell tents. As you can imagine on your first camp, the older boys got preference of where their camping lilo would go. With me being in the younger group we were located beside the tent door, but it didn't bother me, I was just so excited to be away from home, ready for the adventure.

Every morning there was a camp inspection, after breakfast we had to make sure our bell tent was tidy, sleeping bag folded up correctly and dishes, cutlery all washed and presented in the right way.

WILL YOUR ANCHOR HOLD

There was a competition for the best tent for the camp, this involved team games, teamwork, good behaviour and of course the daily inspections for being tidy and cleanliness. We were part of a team, this made us aware that it was not about the individual, but we were now part of a team, making us responsible for each other. I found this easy and actually embraced and enjoyed the extra bit of responsibility. However for one or two of the other young guns, this was not easy, and my best friend was often in trouble, either with the dreaded bog duty, which involved digging a massive hole to get rid of the toilet waste. The other punishment was extra dishes duty - washing, drying the dishes, for nearly forty boys and another ten officers, not good fun!

Through the night, there was a tent battle going on, this is what I loved and was good at it too, due to being a fast runner and light on my feet. The object was to pull all the guy ropes out and the tent would fall down, making for some angry noises and much swearing coming from those in the tent that had now collapsed. This was a nightly occurrence and I was usually the one delegated by my tent commander to go out and bring down the so-called enemy. One night, I had just pulled out the second guy rope peg, and the commander from the other tent came flying out and believe this, threw a wooden mallet at me, it just whistled pass my left

WILL YOUR ANCHOR HOLD

ear, if this had hit me, then it could have easily killed me- mental!

Back then I didn't cause a scene, I just ran back into my sleeping bag, with my slowly leaking lilo, yes, the dreaded lilo leaking, and when morning came it was totally flat. My tip for camping, don't scrimp and buy the cheapest lilo, buy the best so you know that you will get a full night's sleep. I think the only downside to the Boys Brigade camps was the lack of quality sleep, and ten nights on a lilo, especially a leaking one, did take its toll.

The days were action packed, sometimes going for a long walk, we did walk to the Old Man of Hoy from camp, and I loved it. What a truly remarkable sight, seeing the Old Man of Hoy from the cliff edge. It was a long walk, but doing it with friends and having fun, laughter on the way, made the experience a joyful one.

There was a burn that ran through Rackwick, another beautiful addition to the camp, and it was deep enough to run from the bank and jump into, it was very cold though. On a hot summer day, nearly all the boys took a dip and we had canoes as well, so we were never bored.

On dry land, there was of course football, rounders, badminton. Inside the large marquee where we had our meals, if it was raining, there were plenty of board games to keep us entertained.

WILL YOUR ANCHOR HOLD

In Rackwick, there is a fantastic bothy which is open to the public, yet we would take it over for our camp. It had a lovely stone fireplace inside, to keep us warm in the evenings. The Bothy was also used for the tuck shop, all the boys had their spending book, and this was supposed to be used daily and wisely. For most of the boys our spending habits were not wise, and most of us were skint by the end of the camp.

Night times were a good time for the boys, we had our hot chocolate and a couple of digestive biscuits, either round a campfire or in the Bothy if the weather was not good.

We all love a laugh, and this one was at my expense, it was my second camp in Rackwick, and again the weather had been fantastic. Well on the Sunday of the camp the parents were invited over to see their boys before they arrived. We had all been swimming in the burn, we were told to get out, dry ourselves down because our parents had arrived. I got dried off in the bell tent and had a towel around my waist while hanging my swimming trunks outside. One of my friend's pulled at my towel, by this time all the Parents heard the commotion and were looking over just as I had trip backwards over the tent guy rope. With hands flying to get my balance, the towel dropped and yes, I was naked in front of all the parents, mine included. I was back in the tent within a second, embarrassed to come out again, just hearing all the laughter outside.

WILL YOUR ANCHOR HOLD

Thankfully I soon recovered and made light of it, that's one thing that came easy to me.

On your first camp, there was the famous initiation, called walk the plank. It was a plank of wood, and the boy who was blind folded had to stand on the plank. Then you felt like you were being lifted into the air, and when the dreaded "JUMP" was yelled, then jump we did. Unknown to the blindfolded boy, the plank was only a few inches of the ground. Many a laugh watching it happen, not so funny being the boy on the plank. There was one lad who knew the score, and he was actually lifted high, but he just casually walked off the plank - he was so fortunate that he didn't injure himself.

Dornoch Boys Brigade camp was ace, weather, the location, and the year made for a wonderful camp. Sunshine every day in the beautiful town of the Dornoch in the Highlands of Scotland, and the scenery was stunning, such a beautiful place.

The campsite was right beside the local football pitch, so a massive bonus, many of the boys played football, and with the great weather, the football players had a fantastic time. With the year being 1982, the World Cup was on in Spain. I think by the time we were at camp, Scotland had already been knocked out. We had beaten New Zealand 5-2, then lost to the amazing Brazil team, but who can forget that famous goal by David Narey, greatest toe poke ever. In the final game Scotland had to beat the

WILL YOUR ANCHOR HOLD

USSR, the game finished 2-2, so Scotland were out. Looking back, the Scotland team were a brilliant group of players, but yet again failed at the group stage. At least the Scottish team always qualified back then, from 1974 through to 1990 Scotland would qualify for a World Cup.

Dornoch had everything going for it, and we loved the ice-cream shop in the town, owned by an Italian man, the name of the shop was Luigi`s. The highlight of visiting this shop was when Italy knocked out Brazil, we were in the shop when Paolo Rossi scored the winner, 3-2 to Italy, with Rossi scoring a hat trick. The owner went mental celebrating, shouting "Gooooaaaal", and other things in Italian, he ran out the shop waving his arms, then came back into the shop and gave us free ice cream, what a memory!

There was a Boys Brigade company up from Edinburgh, they were good lads and we had fun with them, even took them on at a football match, my best friend who actually played for them and scored his own hat trick, just like Paolo Rossi lol.

We thought our Boys Brigade officers were strict until we witnessed what the Edinburgh boys had to do if their behaviour was not good. One of the Edinburgh boys had to run around the football pitch just in his pants carrying a gas cylinder. Just imagine that happening now!

WILL YOUR ANCHOR HOLD

The only downside to that camp was some fighting with the locals. There was a couple of fisty cuffs going on, and the Police were involved, thankfully no arrests, just a warning to some the boys.

Now onto the camp in Peebles…again when were blessed with the weather, wall to wall sunshine, and in another beautiful location, whoever picked these locations certainly knew what they were doing. The only problem for me and a couple of the other boys was the travel sickness, from being on the boat from Stromness to Thurso, then the long journey on the bus, the travel sickness was not nice, had to stop the bus a couple of times to be sick and get much needed fresh air.

The memories from this camp were the football match against the German boy scouts who were also on our camp site. We ran circles around this team, and I was on fire, at the age of 15, running at speed and the close ball control was my major asset, so this game was very enjoyable. The only negative from the match was that one of the Boys in the Stromness Company had this obsession with anything dare I say it, Nazi. He had been to one of the Army shops in Edinburgh and bought German swastika`s. While playing football against the German team, the swastika`s had fallen out his pocket, myself and a couple of the team quickly jumped on the swastika`s and thankfully the German lads did not notice, or if they did, nothing was said, thank goodness.

WILL YOUR ANCHOR HOLD

With being one of the oldest at the camp, myself and a friend were tent commanders, we shared this responsibility over the ten days. For the last inspection of the camp, our tent and the tent with who you could call a prefect for the Boys Brigade were all square and nothing could decide us, so it came down to the morning inspection to decide the winner. With it being so hot, someone, yes me, had went for a drink and I forgot to dry the inside on my cup, so when the officers came to inspect, yes you got it, they found a plate with water on it, from my dripping cup. As you imagine, I would not be able to live this down for a few days.

The highlight of the Peebles camp was our exciting visit to Ibrox Park, Glasgow. Now as a blue nose, along with a few of the other boys, this was awesome. We were given the tour around the famous stadium, trophy room, changing rooms and out the tunnel. We were not allowed on the pitch; it was getting prepared for the season ahead. Even back then in the early 80s, Ibrox was a magnificent stadium. All the players were away on hols, well so we thought, until I heard my best friend say, "Is that Davie Cooper ?!", and it was. This was the icing on the cake. You see, Davie Cooper was my favourite player, I had a huge poster above my bed of Super Cooper, so to now meet him in the flesh, was a dream come true. Davie came over to chat with us, he was a gentleman and signed autographs, took time to chat and made sure he chatted to everyone.

WILL YOUR ANCHOR HOLD

One of my friends did not have paper or an autograph book, so he asked Davie to sign the elastic band on his swimming googles, brilliant memories.

The spirit of adventure was and still is in me, and there were plenty opportunities for me and my friends growing up in Stromness. Football in my early teens was the focal point, something I did excel at, my first medal and Cup Final was the Boys Brigade 1978, and from then it was win, win, win. Winning the Junior League with Stromness, the first win in a long time was a superb achievement and we had a really good side.

I remember that we had to get a point against our Thorfinn, who were our main rivals. We were away from home in Kirkwall, and we knew that it would be a tough match. We were 2-0 nil down, and looking like we would lose, then we pulled a goal back. In the last few minutes, we were awarded a free-kick and the lad with the rocket shot in our team, scored an absolute screamer, right in the top corner. The match finished 2-2 and Stromness were the Champions. During this match I was conversing with the God, saying "Lord, if we get the right result then I will follow you". As we know, the Lord is not to be bargained with, but these were the moments when I would acknowledge that there was a higher power, even though I was asking from a selfish point of view. Anyway, after the final whistle, I of course soon put that conversion into a distant memory, quickly getting back to the normal routine of life.

My bedtime routine did involve prayer, and I made this a consistent habit for the years ahead, usually asking forgiveness for the stupid things I was up too.

From 1978 to 1986, I won the Boys Brigade Cup, Stromness Junior league, Stromness B league, played for the Stromness A team at the age of fifteen. The highlight was getting a man of the match against the guy who was the Captain of Orkney, I marked him out of the match. We won the indoor league too, Stromness went unbeaten that season in the indoor league, again what a team.

Youth Club, Stromness won this a couple of times in Orkney, so went onto represent them in the national Youth Club competitions, in Edinburgh at the Meadowbank Stadium and also the Bells Sports Centre in Perth.

Many folks were saying I would go on and make the grade as a football player, along with a Stromness teammate, who was a goal machine, he was an unbelievable talent. Anyway, my Stromness teammate`s mum had booked him into a football camp down in England, it was the Alan Mullery soccer school, and asked me to come along. Well, now the big disappointment, my Dad was not for me going, and after much pleading and shouting, he would not budge. This is something I struggled to

WILL YOUR ANCHOR HOLD

forgive my dad for, this created a big fracture in our relationship, with my dream ripped away from me. The Stromness teammate would go to this camp and he was awarded a Gold trophy, only a couple of the guys from the camp would be awarded the Gold Trophy, a brilliant achievement.

When he came back home to Orkney after the Soccer camp, he was on a high and delighted to have the Gold Trophy. I have to admit I was slightly jealous and felt heartbroken that I was not allowed to go to this camp. We both had a friendly rivalry through the football, he was the goal scorer and I was the midfielder with the skill and energy as the centre midfielder. On the pitch, we had a great understanding through much practice together, always kicking a ball about to improve our abilities.

Not going to that soccer camp was a massive regret, and I still don't understand why Dad stood in my way, because he had the resources to make it possible. It took me a while to forgive him, and just thinking about it would make me angry.

One other thing we did in Stromness was skateboarding. I loved the skateboard, and with Stromness having plenty of great hills and roads to have fun on the skateboards, I just had to watch out for the traffic. In general it was safe, we could hear or see cars coming from the distance, and there were not many scary moments, well apart from my best

WILL YOUR ANCHOR HOLD

friend nearly getting crushed by the Minister's car lol.

With Stromness having three piers, we spent many a time down at the harbour, and we enjoyed fishing from the pier, or under the pier too. Looking back, this was crazy, because we would go under the pier where the main ferry would berth. With the ship docking, me and my friends would be under the pier, standing just a few feet away from the propeller, that was whirling around. If we had fallen in, then we were dead, would have been sliced into little pieces. Crazy when I look back, and I certainly did not share this with my parents.

When I was on my bike, which was the awesome Grifter bike, I was showing off to a couple of girls, trying to jump across a right angle where the piers met. I never made the jump and landed in the water with my bike, what an embarrassment. Thankfully that day, there were divers in the harbour basin, who kindly retrieved my bike!

Yes, what adventures I had in my youth, so many memories. For the most part all good ones too, an all action time back in the late 70s and early 80s, a time where risk assessment was unheard of. There is so much more I could have shared, but I have written about the ones that were the highlights of a wonderful childhood with my friends.

WILL YOUR ANCHOR HOLD

CHAPTER 6- THE GAME CHANGER

This autobiography has a sports theme running through it, with football at the top of the list, so the title to this chapter will make sense going forward.

We are all on a journey in this life, our time on earth is full of ups and downs, regrets and so on….

Stromness, Orkney was the sure foundation to who I would become in life. Back in the late 70s and early 80s I was hardly ever inside, and even the start of the TV game console would not keep me indoors. Now into my mid-teens the world around me was changing, and, more to the point, I was changing into a young man, and all the testosterone that goes with it.

Home life was much the same, Dad`s mood would be okay for a wee while, then it would all kick off again, with the shouting, swearing and me not wanting to be at home. Dad was also starting to get restless and he was talking about moving to Aberdeen, so I should have heeded the early warning talk about Aberdeen. Mum was still this easy-going lady who made time for her three boys, she loved having us around her, this was Mum`s happy place, and she made us top priority.

The Levi shop in Kirkwall was still a successful business, but dad was not in a happy place, grumpy and restless with everything. It was during this time that he decided to move the shop to Stromness, but

WILL YOUR ANCHOR HOLD

this was a bad move and he realised that the footfall in the West side of the island was much less than the capital, Kirkwall. He then moved the shop back to Kirkwall, to a different location, and by now someone else was starting to sell Levi clothes in Kirkwall. The momentum for their Levi shop had changed and business was quieter, making dad even more frustrated.

My middle brother had also left school, and, with having a disability, work was obviously going to be hard to find. My parents had to place him at a place called St Colms day centre, a place for adults with learning disabilities. He did seem to enjoy it, and the bus would collect him every morning and then take him home from Kirkwall.

My oldest brother had a good life, and was busy taxi driving in the evenings, this was on top of his day job in Kirkwall. He loved playing in the pool league as well, so he was often down at the local pub called the Braes Hotel, brushing up on his pool skills.

For me, I could sense and feel the changes going on within myself, family and even friendships. It is true, nothing stays the same, even though it might look that way. With school exams coming up too I was struggling with all the work, and rather than stick in and study, I did the opposite and became lazy with schoolwork. This meant I was falling behind in the academic field, so I just kind of gave up and started to go through the motions at school.

WILL YOUR ANCHOR HOLD

Football was the highlight, my safe place in life, if you are good at something then it will be a good escape when life becomes hard. I could keep the ball in the air for a long time, and my keepie up record was over 3,000, could have probably done more, but it can be boring lol.

Friday night was starting to become my favourite night, still going to the Boys Brigade, and doing all the crazy things, from Murder Ball to British Bull Dogs, good things to do to release the testosterone at the end of the school week. It was after Boys Brigade that the game changer was about to happen. A few friends and I would start going to our former Boys Brigade Captain's home, where we got plenty of juice, biscuits and an unlimited supply of tea/coffee. His home was home 24/7, and many folks would walk in and unload their life's problems to this guy. He was, and still is, a fantastic man with a huge heart for his community, and being a born-again Christian he has a great nature and a wonderful caring side.

It was these Friday nights that would introduce me to Jesus, the place where the call of God on my life would awaken. After the initial juice, biscuits etc our former Captain from the Boys Brigade would chat about his faith and he would get the guitar out and start singing worship songs. He was a wonderful communicator too, so he made the Bible stories come to life and sound exciting just by his story-telling skills.

WILL YOUR ANCHOR HOLD

Most of my friends were not interested in the 'God stuff' as they would call it, and they felt uncomfortable and embarrassed by it all. For me, I could not get enough, and I would start firing questions about all things God/Faith. Looking back, the Holy Spirit was working in my life and my heart would start to flutter and pump harder when anything of Jesus was shared. Even then I could feel and sense that there was a battle going on, the unseen battle for a young man's soul.

It says in Galatians chapter 5 verse 17, "for the flesh desires what is contrary to the Spirit, and the Spirit what is contrary to the flesh. They are in conflict with each other, so that you are not to do whatever you want" (NIV). The apostle Paul who wrote this letter in the New Testament is describing in this verse that there is a conflict that goes on in the heart and mind of every Christian.

Well, I was not even a Christian then, and I could feel the pull on my heart, spirit and of course the mind. The heart was stirring, and my spirit man was starting to awaken, but the mind was elsewhere, it was saying "What are you doing Ricky? You don't need this stuff, it will stop your fun".

Fun, yes that is what we all chase, even now at the age of 53 I love having fun, but back then, life had to be lived, and I wanted to taste what the world had on offer. The Friday routine became Boys Brigade, then onto our former BB Captain's home to have

WILL YOUR ANCHOR HOLD

some fun, but for me, mainly to ask more questions about faith and this man Jesus. Back then, we were all introduced to the christian faith, or religion as the majority described it. At Primary school there was the weekly visit from the Minister, he was a good man and full of fun, and he could engage the class by his personality, singing ability and storytelling. There was never any awkwardness with Christianity in the Primary school. However the Academy was a different atmosphere, most of the youth had nothing to do with Church/Christianity, there was a few, but they tended to come from Christian families.

In the Academy you are finding out who are, and everything is changing, your body, attitude, the voice is starting to break, and you want to belong to a similar group or tribe, to feel part of something.

With my parents having a business, and financially well off, I guess looking back I was treated differently, but I didn't know this back then. Status and money do make a huge difference, and you cannot really argue against the fact that people are more respected who have a so-called status and financial clout. You are unaware of this when you have the status and finances, it's only when you are out this way of life, that your eyes are opened to this superficial world.

The Levi kid was shouted about "here`s Bain the Levi kid" or "here`s the little poser" or even worse usually. Most of the comments were in fun, but

WILL YOUR ANCHOR HOLD

there was of course a few with a sting in them. In Orkney, the boys are mostly called by their surname, so Bain was my usual name, and I wasn't averse to this. In my mid-teens I was confident in who I was, and in fact like a lot of young men, a bit too cocky for my own good. I didn't have a bad bone in my body, I got on with most folks and always made sure I made eye contact and said hello to everyone I met.

There is a popular crowd in all schools, in fact there is a popular crowd no matter where you are; schools, workplaces and even in the church and it was no different in the 80s. For me, it was a case of, yes, I admire those in the school who have a faith in Jesus, but they all seem different and don't connect with the friends I have. They also were of the higher academic group, and I could not see myself sitting in a circle with a bible open, discussing the deep, theological themes in the Bible. Even then, I knew I would never be a scholar of the good book, and I mean this with no disrespect to the higher intellectual ones who love to study scripture.

I was reminded too, that back in the Primary days, there were many kids who attended the St John's Gospel hall in Stromness on a Sunday afternoon, these were brilliantly run, a fast paced environment, with team games, quizzes and singing, also plenty of juice and snacks. The folks who ran these afternoons certainly knew how to connect with the kids and made the Christian adventure exciting too.

WILL YOUR ANCHOR HOLD

If any of you are reading now, then please take a bow, you did well and made a positive difference to me and to many others. Even to those who might not admit to it!

They also did football and cricket at the market green on a Saturday morning, which was brilliant fun, and I think they enjoyed getting to run alongside the youth and having fun themselves.

The reality is that in the late 70s and early 80s we had a lot of exposure to Christianity, with an active church, St John`s Gospel hall, the Minister at the schools, Boys Brigade, Sunday School picnics and of course for me, my Friday nights too.

God was gently introducing himself to me, yet I had my parents against it, and my friends had no time for it, probably due to their family culture too. When the Holy Spirit is on you, it's hard to get away from it, but God is a gentleman, and will not force Himself on you, He invites you to make a personal choice.

Life was full on, and even though I loved my Friday nights, for me, there was just too much good fun to had, and I thought to myself "I`ll make peace with God later, sure he understands".

There was a night at our former BB Captains house that still comes strongly to my thoughts even now, I remember this night so well….there was me and a couple of friends at the house, just chilling, drinking

WILL YOUR ANCHOR HOLD

juice, tea/ coffee and of course plenty of biscuits. When all of a sudden four older boys appeared, now this was a huge surprise, these lads were in the late teens, early 20s, and were typical Orkney boys as you would say. They liked to party, and of course loved their cars. They were not in to cause trouble, this was evident, they came in and had a drink, and ate plenty of biscuits. Before we knew it, they were asking the host all about God and who this Jesus guy was, they were serious too, and we had some really good, honest conversations about the Lord.

The reason this night is embedded in my thoughts and heart, is not long after that evening, there was a fatal car crash in Orkney, and one of the young guys who was at the house was killed in that horrific crash. One of the questions from that night at the house was about eternity and life beyond our natural life, and these boys acknowledged that there was a God, but in their own words "I believe there is a God, but I will make peace with my maker later in life, too much living to do now".

That couple of years in Orkney, there were so many deaths from car crashes, and this created so much heart broken families, it was devastating for such a small community. Even then, living amongst the devastation, I, like most folks, thought I was immortal and nothing would happen to me.

Walking home one beautiful night, the starts were absolutely mesmerising, and I could sense God all

WILL YOUR ANCHOR HOLD

around me, like he was right beside me, could feel the tug on my heart. I knew all I had to say was "Lord, you are my saviour, please forgive me for all the bad/ stupid things I have done in my life, I now confess you as my Lord and Saviour". These words were floating around in my mind, but I just could not verbalise this life changing statement, it was like another force was blocking the signal from the head to the heart.

Looking back, I do reflect on what my life could have been if I had obeyed the Holy Spirit and asked Jesus into my life. I'm sure there would have been less heartbreak and more direction, wisdom into the equation. God knows the beginning to the end, and he is a God of love, patience and never gives up on anyone!

For the next two years, from the age of 15-17 years, I chased after all that this world can offer, and chasing the girls became a passion too. The mid-teens are when the house parties started to happen, and I was in this crowd, where many of the youth had already started smoking, drinking etc.
Thankfully even then I was not a heavy drinker, might have had the odd tin of cider and a couple of beers, but with football still my dream, I was really fit and looked after my body.

Of course, there was a few nights with having one drink to many, but in general I was not influenced by drink then. This of course would change going

WILL YOUR ANCHOR HOLD

forward. With drink, parties and lots of teenage hormones and emotions kicking in, then as you can imagine, there was all sorts of shenanigans going on, and I did enjoy female company.

Young men back in the 80s were not the most comfortable or romantic around the girls, this goes back to not being taught or shown how to treat the opposite sex. For me, I look back with huge regret in how I treated girls, and hope and pray that my son will treat the ladies much better than I did. Girlfriends back then, there was two girls that I did care for, and also had real feelings too. I just wasn't ready to give my whole time to a girl.

The *game changer*, yes, the move to Aberdeen, this all became more evident when one morning I heard the front door being slammed, I came through the house and saw that mum was upset. She said "Dad's had enough and is away on the boat to Aberdeen". You know, hearing these words, part of me was glad, deep down I knew what was going to happen next, with all the talk of moving to Aberdeen. I thought, good, if Dad goes then I can stay in Stromness. Later that day, Dad called Mum on the phone, and she seemed to be happy that Dad had calmed down. A couple of days later, they both were down in Aberdeen, looking for a house, it was real, it was serious, we were going to move!

Ibrox was now up for sale, aye the Orkney one, not Glasgow. Sadly I knew it was happening and that

WILL YOUR ANCHOR HOLD

Ibrox would sell quickly due to its location, with amazing views over Stromness, the Hoy hills and over Scapa Flow. I didn't realise back then that we stayed in one of the most wonderful locations in Stromness, yep, we certainly do take life for granted until it is gone.

Getting my head around leaving was tough, but I had to start dealing with it. Thankfully I had the Orkney junior football to keep me focused for my last couple of months, and I trained harder than ever. My daily routine was 100 sit ups, 100 press ups and lots of running or cycling, this was a consistent daily routine, and boy was I fit. There was a girl who I had become very close too, she stayed in Kirkwall and I did my best to get through to visit her. The last few weeks were difficult for me, lots of tears and saying goodbye to my close friends and family. The Levi shop was now sold, Ibrox had been sold and my parents had bought a house in Aberdeen, my oldest brother had now moved into a flat in Stromness.

My folks moved in May 1986 to Aberdeen with my middle brother. I was to stay with my oldest brother so that I could play the last inter county game against Caithness. I remember my last night in Stromness, walking around the town where I had lived and grown, there was tears flowing to my cheeks and I thought, why am I leaving this town, it's part of me, I belong here.

WILL YOUR ANCHOR HOLD

Again looking back, I should have been stronger, and dug my heals in to stay but I obeyed my parents and honoured them. In early June 1986 on a warm summer's day I arrived to my new abode. Driven to Aberdeen with my oldest brother, we arrived at a nice location, 66 Leggart Terrace would be my home for the next nine years. The house itself was stunning, with a huge garden out the back, Dad looked happy and Mum was glad to keep him happy, which of course was wrong.

WILL YOUR ANCHOR HOLD

CHAPTER 7- OUT OF CONTROL

Now here I was, basically in a foreign land, coming from a place where nearly everyone knew who I was, to being a nobody.

Meeting new people and having to make an effort to be noticed was something I was good at, but it was just weird not being part of a community or a fabric of society that I had been immersed in.

School exam results had not been good, this was not a shock for me, the last couple of years at school had felt wasted on the academic side. I loved the social and sports, but my results were a huge let down, and I felt embarrassed and a massive failure.

Dad was at me to get a job, my heart was to go to Telford Collage in Edinburgh, to do a course in Sport and Fitness. I still believe to this day that I should have stood my ground and went for it. Aye but I did the honourable son thing and started looking for a job, yes any job would do, to get Dad off my back.

After a couple of months just dossing about Aberdeen, I got a job in a supermarket, owned by Fine Fare, about two miles from where we lived. My job was in the in-store butchery department, my job title was Meat Assistant. This role was like a general assistant in the butchery department; to pack the meat, make sure the store display cabinet was well stocked up and be the labourer in the

WILL YOUR ANCHOR HOLD

department. This was of course a huge shock to my system, and I soon realised how cruel people can be in the real world.

My working week was from Monday to Saturday with every Sunday off, and alternative days off as the weeks progressed. So, I got the occasional Saturday off, which for my football journey was devastating, since the local juvenile league was played on the Saturday.

Coming from a place of where I could play football every day to having nothing was like my world had ended, only those of you have played football will understand that statement. You see, before I got the job at Fine Fare, I was training with the Cove Rangers youth team and doing well. Now because I had a job, meaning Saturday was out, I had to look elsewhere.

There was a difference to the football too, going from being one of the first picked in the team to being last, because I didn`t know anyone. Now I would know how it felt hearing names being said before mine, and being the last one standing was not a nice feeling. I was getting flash backs to all those sad faces I had seen growing up, now I could feel their hurt.

The Stoneywood Juvenile team was my next destination, a good side and they made me welcome, but again due to missing most Saturdays this became impossible to carry on. Their manager

WILL YOUR ANCHOR HOLD

at the time offered me a painting apprenticeship to help me stay in football, but again I followed advice from Dad who said, "You have a job, be thankful".

As you can imagine, the weeks and months passed and I was so unhappy and thought, is this what the world has to offer? I was thinking "I should have stuck in at school, I should have been brave and went to Edinburgh".

The manager of the butcher department was not the easiest guy to get on with, and was impatient too, with a temper to match. The other two butchers were okay, and they were up for some banter, especially if the manager was on his day off, these days I enjoyed. At the end of the working week the conversations turned to what was happening at the weekends, well with no football I was up for some fun and a chance to maybe get away from the mundane life I was now part off. The bright city lights of the Aberdeen nightlife, for a boy from the islands and with an eye for the ladies, this made for a crazy few years of weekends out.

Yes, my weekend would now be getting drunk, chasing the ladies and over the next few years I would be a regular in the city centre. You see, I could not handle that I had a job which did nothing for me, and a manager who did not have time for me, even though (looking back) I didn't help myself with a poor attitude and an obvious dislike for my job.

WILL YOUR ANCHOR HOLD

Home life was bearable, but Dad was still flaring up and Mum trying to keep the peace. She was a remarkable lady, and had so much grace for her husband. Dad was now working harder than ever and not doing (what I looked at as) the good things he did back in Orkney - gone was the golf, darts and the good social life they had in Stromness.

Now here he was working seven days a week, with no time to enjoy what he loved doing, it, still baffles me to this day. Don't get me wrong, he was wonderful to my middle brother and my parent's routine on a Saturday evening was taking him for a couple of beers, their love for all the boys was evident. It's only now being a parent that I have any inkling as to what they had to persevere with in looking after my middle brother 24/7, these are pressures that would test a saint.

With their focus and time on my middle brother, well I just started to treat the house like a hotel, coming and going as I pleased. With now coming home in the early hours at the weekend or often not coming home, then the friction started, and I do not blame my parents for this. I was getting drunk and I had now started something I never thought I would ever do, yes I had begun to smoke, not good. With going out every weekend I had become a social smoker, which had maybe been one night a week, unfortunately my weekends were now three to four nights a week.

WILL YOUR ANCHOR HOLD

One morning I was in the kitchen and saw my dad's cigarettes on the table, I took a fag and lit it up, on my way to work I bought a packet and so began my full time smoking career. For the next few years my routine would be work, then party and this became a lifestyle that would lead me to spending all my money on alcohol and cigarettes, not clever and certainly not wise.

I made a good friend while working at Gateway, he was good fun and we did a lot of partying together. One night though I was in the back seat of his Ford Escort Mexico, it was a beautiful car, he was driving, and his girlfriend was in the passenger seat, an era when seatbelts were not being worn. We were traveling on the back road from Altens to Torry, and going fast… there was a big bend ahead, the car was going far too fast, I could feel the car sliding out of control. My friend tried to correct it by quickly turning the steering, but the car hit the big kerb , which caused the car to flip over, the car flipped over twice, and I remember going down the road while the car was on its roof, it felt like slow motion. Thankfully the car came to a stop, we all realised that no one was hurt, my friend's girlfriend was hysterical, and no wonder. I got out the back window, every bit of glass was smashed, the car was a mess, and it was a miracle that no one was hurt.

The next day my friend and I went to the scrapyard to see his car, there were two Police officers in front

WILL YOUR ANCHOR HOLD

of us conversing, one said "That car is destroyed, there is not a chance that anyone survived that crash". We shouted out "we are right behind you, and thankfully still alive".

This was my second car crash, my first was when we were on holidays in Edinburgh, my Dad was driving that day, and an MG Midget came right into the side of us, again no seatbelts on, and we were all okay. I will share about the other two car crashes in the later chapters.

The staff in Gateway were good people, I got friendly with one of the bakers, we had a common interest in football, especially Glasgow Rangers. I played 5 a-side once a week with my work mates and this was very enjoyable.

On the Glasgow Rangers front, my baker pal had contacts in Glasgow and asked if I would fancy going to an Old Firm match. I had been to a Final at Hampden against Celtic, which Rangers won. This one would be at Parkhead, an away match, I was up for it, and we travelled down to Glasgow to meet his contacts in a pub. Well I should have heeded the warning signs when my friend`s mate said "guys you will need to leave your scarfs here!", the tickets that we got were for the Celtic end. We already had drunk a few beers, so the drink is in and the wit is out, yes before I knew it, I was in the ground in the away end and surrounded by Celtic fans, those were the days of standing, so crammed in like sardines.

WILL YOUR ANCHOR HOLD

The year was 1988, Celtic scored after five minutes and everyone around us went crazy, the place was going mental, there were ten blue noses in the middle of this madness. I was petrified and made even worse when Graeme Souness was sent off, which increased the already passionate atmosphere. Rangers did score, but the goal was chopped off for offside, didn't stop my mate jumping around and shouting stupid things to the Celtic fans, thankfully the stewards surrounded us for our own protection, and we were escorted out of the ground. I've never been so delighted to be leaving a football match, looking back it was a crazy thing to do, utter stupidity.

I spent four years at the supermarket, which was now owned by the supermarket chain called Gateway. Thankfully I managed to get a job in the oil industry in 1990.

Before I go to share about the oil industry job, I did apply to be a fire-fighter in the RAF. I passed the exam, but failed my medical : I am technically blind in my left eye, so I failed on eyesight. I was gutted! Looking back I could have passed, because back then you were asked to cover your opposite eye with your hand. I have a bend on my right index fingers, so could see out my good eye. However I was honest and did not use this to my benefit. The other thing that annoyed me that day, was that there was a lad down from Shetland who was way overweight, and I was probably in my prime

WILL YOUR ANCHOR HOLD

physically. The nurse said that we can`t do nothing with your eye, but we can get the guy from Shetland fit for action. As I said, I was devastated, actually fuming, life can be brutal, so unfair. My mum was delighted though, she didn`t want her baby boy to leave home.

When I arrived in Aberdeen in 1986, there was a huge downturn in the Oil industry, but by 1990 it had picked up again. I found myself working as a yardman with a company in Dyce. I did like this job and with working Monday to Friday, I could now go back to playing football on a Saturday.

For the football, I had got to Junior level, which is a decent level of football, and managed to play at that level even though I worked a lot of Saturday`s with my previous job. In fact, I was playing football on a Saturday and Sunday, often getting a lift from a good friend on a Sunday morning. I was still drunk from the night before, and he often collected me from various locations on a Sunday morning.

With having my Saturday`s back I now played in the Premier division of the amateur league, with a team called West End, a very good footballing team, and a brilliant team spirit, also of course back in the day, a team who would party together. So now it was work, football and still much partying to do, and with my work, I did enjoy what I was doing. Yet, the more money I made, the more nights out I went on.

WILL YOUR ANCHOR HOLD

Now the night that changed everything, to this day I will never forget what happened on Nov 25th, 1993…

That night I had a knee injury so could not go to football training, and I spent the night playing cards with my mum, we had so much fun and laughter that evening. Little did I know that this would be the last time we would talk, since at 4am on Thursday the 25th November my mum suffered a massive heart attack. Dad had woken up the house shouting- "Sylvia, Sylvia what is wrong", then he ran down stirs to call the ambulance. By this time, I was in their bedroom, holding my mum has she passed away. The paramedics arrived and ushered us out the room, they tried everything to bring her back, as she was taken away in the ambulance, deep down I knew that my beautiful mum had passed away.

Dad followed the ambulance in the car, and a couple of hours later he was home to confirm that mum had died, devastating for all those left behind. You know, this is one of only two times I saw my dad cry, he was heartbroken. The lovely lady who I called mum was now gone. She was the cornerstone of the home, the homemaker, an amazing wife to my dad and a wonderful mum to three boys.

As the weeks passed the atmosphere in the house was fragile at best, poor dad was totally lost, and my brother and I were still processing the loss. At that time of my life, my default was to turn to drink, and

WILL YOUR ANCHOR HOLD

this I did every weekend without fail. I got absolutely hammered week after week. I managed to get into a few scuffles too, and my friends were concerned say "This is not you Ricky, what is wrong?"

You know, I was hurting for the loss of my mum, and had nowhere to go to speak out my grief and heart ache. Dad was dealing with the loss of his wife, he was not in a place to chat and didn't know how to deal with this life-changing event. Thank goodness there is more awareness these days for men to chat about the deeper stuff in life, because guys are not the best chatting about their emotions.

About a year after mum had passed, I moved to a flat near the Bridge of Don, this allowed a for a better relationship with dad, it was time I had moved anyway. Looking back, I had stayed too long at home, but felt the need to be there for mum, like a protector I suppose! The flat was freedom in some ways, yet isolation too, with still working, partying and playing football, no change to my lifestyle.

One evening, my mood was extremely low, and there were many dark thoughts leading up to what I was about to do, I felt useless, hopeless. Before I knew it, I had tied a rope that I had bought a couple of days before around the joist, took the kitchen stool over. Then I stood on the stool, put the rope around my neck and kicked away the stool, I could feel myself passing out, thankfully something

WILL YOUR ANCHOR HOLD

kicked in, I reached out my foot to the stool, managed to stand up again, the rope was off in seconds. What a horrible mental state I must have had at that time, the death of my mum was indeed life changing for me, and my coping mechanism was drink, not a wise combination.

I went to work and football training the next day, making up silly excuses for the marks on my neck, what a dark place where my mind had gone.

Now as I close this chapter, let me bring in the God factor… not long after I had attempted to commit suicide, I was on yes, another night out in the town. That evening there was a team of people on the streets in Aberdeen, handing out flyers, the team had arrived that day on a ship called the *MV Logos* working under Operation Mobilisation. One of the team had handed my friend a flyer, he automatically threw it over his shoulder, then I coolly picked it up off the pavement and put the flyer in my pocket. When I woke up the next morning, there was the usual change in my pockets and I pulled out the flyer which had *Jesus Your Saviour* on it. Suddenly that same feeling I had in my heart as a teenager stirred again.

Jeremiah 29 v11 For I know the plans I have for you," declares the LORD, "plans to prosper you and not to harm you, plans to give you hope and a future".

WILL YOUR ANCHOR HOLD

CHAPTER 8- NO ONE LOVES LIKE JOANNE

Now from the day my mum died in November 1993 to 1996 was obviously (looking back) traumatic for me, my dad, and my brothers. With only having males left in a family after the mother has gone, the communication was limited. With mum passing away, there was a massive emotional void in the Bain family.

Mum was my sounding board, and since she had passed away then I had no one who would listen to all my problems or moans the way she could. She was my biggest ally, our relationship was strong, authentic and full of love. 'That's the way it should be with a mother and child relationship' will be your thoughts as you read this, but I know many who do not have a relationship with their mums, let alone a good one.

Amongst all the pain, hurt and (I'll say how it is) chaos in my life, I still prayed every night to God, probably out of habit and not relationship, and usually to ask for forgiveness for the way I had lived. When I had stayed at home in Leggart Terrace in Aberdeen, I am ashamed to say that I used to steal money from my mum's handbags. She had them stored in a cabinet in the living room, so every weekend I would steal from her handbags. The money was to feed a habit, yes, I stole to feed my alcohol addiction, there's no other way to describe it.

WILL YOUR ANCHOR HOLD

When you live in shame, feeling hopeless and a failure then it's not a good place to be, you feel worthless and empty. One day I had come home to see dad and to wash my car, it was a gorgeous day, and I was feeling good that day. While washing the car, I saw two nice looking girls approaching, they stopped for a chat and asked various questions about life. They got me thinking about life, and then they said they were Jehovah Witnesses. I knew about the JW`s, I automatically thought I don`t care who or what you believe in, you are attractive.

So, before I knew it, they had arranged to come and see me at my flat, which was on the other side of the town. The two of them came for a few weeks, and they spoke about the *Watchtower* magazine and mostly about the end times, the wrath of God. These visits did make me start to look deeper into all things of God. Over time, there was only one girl who started to come along, now this was wrong, but I thought, well I liked her company and who knows what might happen. These visits did not impact on the way I was living, still partying every weekend, even though a lot of my friends had now settled down and I was beginning to get a bit fed up in going out.

On March Saturday 24th 1996, the day before my 27th Birthday, I was actually thinking about just staying in. At about 18:15 I thought, I`ll phone a friend and if he doesn't answer then I will just stay at home and watch *Blind Date* lol. His phone was

WILL YOUR ANCHOR HOLD

ringing and no answer, I was just about to hang up when he shouted "*Hello*", he had just gone out the door and heard the phone ringing. Well that night I was in the usual Saturday state, yes, very drunk and I had ended up in a nightclub called *Franklyns*, a regular haunt for me. While upstairs I said "Hello" to a girl who walked past and she told me to 'do one', or words to that effect, and then a beautiful girl came up and said "sorry for my friend, she was a bit rude". We got chatting and she said her name was Joanne; something clicked, I was taken by her amazing smile, and her laugh was infectious, and she was easy to chat too.

That night I was chatting to the Aberdeen football team, they were up for a laugh, and one of them had come over to Joanne and said "Here`s 10p, tell your mum you will not be home tonight", yes, a real cheesy one liner.

Within weeks Joanne and I were in each pockets, always together unless working or I was at football training, she had captured my heart. Joanne had a big room in the nursing home accommodation in Aberdeen, and we spent a lot of time there, again our chats were easy conversations and we talked about everything and anything. Joanne was a natural talker, and I found this good, she was a great storyteller, and her lovely accent made this easy listening.

WILL YOUR ANCHOR HOLD

In her room was a Bible, and I would often flick through the pages, asking a lot of questions -God was now stirring my heart and invading my thought life. Joanne had spoken about growing up in Tain and giving her heart to Jesus at the age of 13, but since moving to Aberdeen she had not found a church that she could feel part of.

Joanne at that time was not for talking anything God or the Bible, but she was surprisingly taken aback with my interest in Jesus. Going forward, much of our conversations turned to faith, and we were both comfortable in chatting about it. Slowly but surely, I could see the passion come back into Joanne`s life for Jesus, and on our first trip North to Tain she played some Christian songs on the car stereo, and I was okay with this.

I know Joanne shared in her own book about a certain song that went along these lines "*Teach me to dance to the beat of your heart, teach me to move in the power of your Spirit*", that's a song by Graham Kendrick, a famous Christian song writer. God is in the detail of all our lives, and I knew heading up to Tain to meet Joanne`s family that Joanne was the girl for me, and what a lucky man I was… and I still am!

The closer we got to Tain, the more nervous I got, usually I was relaxed meeting new people, but its different meeting the folks who would become my in-laws. When I arrived at Joanne`s parent`s home, I

WILL YOUR ANCHOR HOLD

walked into the porch and instantly saw many books, the majority of these being of a Christian influence. Her parents were both so welcoming and made me feel at ease right away, they were both so relational and I was soon at ease in their company.

That weekend I must have met the whole family and god parents, yes, there was a lot of new connections and lifelong relationships made that weekend. Over the next few months, we made the trip North a few times and I loved the venture up to my second home, that's what I felt like going to Tain.

One weekend I picked up a book from the mother in-law's big collection, and the book was the Kris Akabusi's autobiography called *Kris Akabusi On Track*. With me loving sport and interested in a story of faith, this was something I wanted to read. So, over the weekend I read most of the book, and Kris's life story had a huge influence on me that weekend.

Joanne and I got engaged after only three months, yes, a quick engagement, but we knew that we were right for one another and our personalities were certainly a match. Joanne's parents did come down to meet my dad, and they got on okay. Dad was a man's man, and my father In-law ticked all the boxes, my mother in-law did well with feeling a bit left out.

At this time I was working at Stoneywood papermill, working a shift rotation. This was called

WILL YOUR ANCHOR HOLD

continental shift`s, these were 12-hour day and night shift, with a lot of time off.

Joanne was only 20 years old and I was 27 years old, looking back I should have been more mature and made life easier for Joanne, hindsight is a great thing though. If Joanne needed the car, she would get up early and take me to work, that was devotion for you, and Joanne would go above and beyond to help out. The papermill years were indifferent, the work was boring, the shift pattern was a good one, with a lot of time off.

Joanne had met me just as I was heading to France to play in a football tournament where all the Arjo Wiggins' papermills would send a football team to compete in the tournament. There were teams from all over the world : Brazil, Germany, Holland, Wales, England and another team from Scotland (Fort William). These tournaments were exciting, competitive and made awesome memories.

I attended four tournaments in total, and we did win the final in France, but it was the semi-final where there were chaotic scenes. We were playing one of the French teams, they had excellent players, but their temperament was shocking. The game was getting dirty, tackles flying everywhere and then all of a sudden I felt this warm stuff running down my neck, one of the French players had just spat on me, I couldn't believe it! The referee, who was from Wales, did not see the incident, but he knew something was amiss due to my reaction, and a few other players saw it too. When I looked at the culprit, he had a huge smile on his face, well that was soon changed.... when the ball was being kicked out by their keeper I knew the ref would be watching the ball. I elbowed the culprit right on his nose, and blood started to pour. I should not have done this, I was always in control of my emotions on the pitch, and even after this game didn't have any issues, I've never been red carded. If the ref had seen what I had done then a straight red would have been given. The ref again knew something had happened and did not see the altercation. The French players were going nuts, and I had to be protected by my team mates, I looked at the French captain and he did the throat cutting sign, so I knew this could escalate. The game went to penalties, and I scored the winning penalty, making me even more popular with the French players!

At night-time there was a brilliant event at a beautiful facility, there was a big band, lots of food, drink and a good atmosphere. Even then I knew that I was a target, and this became evident when I stood up from our table to go to the toilet, the whole French side stood up as well. If I had gone to the toilet myself then who knows what could have happened. As I shared, my reaction on the pitch was wrong, in my favour though was that I had taken bad tackles without reacting, but someone spitting on you is a step too far.

WILL YOUR ANCHOR HOLD

Joanne had some experiences with the French players too - a year later in Aberdeen, I was getting rough treatment on the pitch, kicked all over the pitch. Joanne had had enough, and when the ball went out for a throw in, she gave the French players a mouthful. One of the French players picked up the ball and bounced it off her head. Not a wise thing to do, and the game became another battle.

My highlight of working at the Papermill was playing football, and I got a wee taste of playing football abroad, good memories and fun times too. Joanne has always had a love/hate relationship with football, she doesn't really like the game or the football culture, yet she fell in love with me and adored the ground I walked on.

We both had spoken about getting married, and had decided to go for August 1997, but we could not get time off together, and before we knew it, we were now booked to marry on 21st December 1996 at the Royal Hotel in Tain. Even my friends were saying, 'slow down, you hardly know one another', well, there was no stopping us and we were excited about getting married.

Engaged after three months and now looking to be married in nine months, no messing about, there was much to do, to be fair Joanne did most of the planning and arrangements. With most of our friends under short notice for the wedding, we had it in our minds that many would not make it,

WILL YOUR ANCHOR HOLD

especially with the wedding being just four days before Christmas, it was a big ask for them.

The wedding preparation went well, and we were ready for our big day, many of our wedding guests arrived the night before, and what a party there was at Joanne's folks house that night. It still annoys me to this day that I was sent home before midnight, it's tradition I was told. Even to this day, I hear how good that night was, especially after I had left to go and sleep at Joanne's god parents, who by the way, are the most wonderful couple.

On the wedding day, the weather for that time of the year was beautiful, yet cold all the same, what a day it was, a truly magical day, we were so blessed. Joanne's god parents had good connections in Tain, and their son played in the local pipe band, so were blessed to have a pipe band as well as lovely wedding cars for our big day.

Dad was on form that weekend and it was great to see him in a happy place. The night before the wedding at the Royal Hotel he played his saxophone along with his best friend, who played the accordion, they had both played in a band in their youth. They were brilliant together and the atmosphere they created was a hit with all the guests.

Joanne and I were married by the local minister from the Church of Scotland, he was Joanne's minister from her youth, so she knew him well. I had met him during our marriage course, and he was a good man with a deep faith in the Lord. I had felt like I wasn`t good enough from a few of the congregation at the Church of Scotland, and Joanne had received a letter from a church member to voice his concern about her marrying a non-believer. God had a better plan thankfully.

The tartan I was married in was the Glasgow Rangers tartan, and there is a brilliant photo with nine guys wearing the tartan. 1996 was the year Rangers completed the nine in a row league titles, yes, a good year to get married. The speech was hard for me, all I could think about was my mum not being there to celebrate our wonderful occasion. My emotions got the better of me, and I was a bubbling wreck, not the best speech, and I did not finish what I had intended to share. Now I was married to the most amazing lady, she was stunning as a bride, she made the local Aberdeen paper, the P & J, for bride of the week.

Joanne and I had our honeymoon in a beautiful log cabin in Aviemore, the setting was quite breath-taking, a winter wonderland. The only downside to the honeymoon was that we both came down with a horrendous flu bug, I have had nothing like it, even to this day.

Writing a book is not easy, naming the chapter`s takes time, with much thought and emotions naming them. I have named this chapter *No one loves like*

WILL YOUR ANCHOR HOLD

Joanne, since to me and the many others who know her, will identify with this. Joanne has such a natural lovely nature, with a beautiful heart to go along with it, she has and still does put others before herself, giving her best to all she knows. Joanne's parents are awesome folks, and when you get to meet or get to know Joanne, then you can see that her love and giftings from her dad & mum have passed down the line.

My in-laws are like family too me; both have shown me love, patience, kindness, often undeserved too. I have never felt judged by them, and with losing parents on my journey, they have embraced me like a son. With Joanne coming from such 'good stock' as they say, then it doesn't surprise you that she is who she is, and I was honoured to have become her husband, but at that time did not appreciate the jewel that became my soul partner.

We had done the right thing in the eyes of God by getting married in a church, and having a Christian wedding, recognising that journey together was being guided by the Lord, even though our lives at the time were still a bit chaotic. There was an army of people praying for us without interfering, and looking back, we would both say that these prayers kept us moving forward in his plans for our lives.

I was now back at work in the papermill, Joanne back at nursing, and you know what, we were both feeling unsettled. Joanne had enough of the nursing and took a job in an office with a nursing agency firm, she did enjoy this role. For me, the papermill job was mundane, and I got to the stage of actually hating going to it, especially on a night-shift weekend.

We chatted about what was next, and I had applied for a job up in Orkney within Kirkwall Airport, my heart was to go back, and yes this was selfish, I did not take Joanne's feeling into consideration. With Joanne being who she is, she gave up her good job in Aberdeen to go to a place she did not know and would have no family there too. Wow, even writing this now, makes me realise what an unselfish act she did to make her husband happy.

I moved up first, staying with my best friend's parents, then Joanne came up to stay, we then moved into the house beside the butcher shop that my friend's family owned. The rent was so cheap, these people were, and still are, the salt of the earth, generous folks who were so good to us. We had hoped Joanne would find a job, but just before we had moved to Orkney, Joanne had become pregnant. It was not the plan for then we thought, yet God is in the detail.

Joanne found it impossible to find a job, well who is going to take on a pregnant lady? So this was going to be a hard road for a young mother to be living in a place she did not know. For me it was great to be back home, and I worked at Kirkwall airport as a ground agent. I enjoyed this job too, but there were not enough hours of employment. Thankfully I managed to get another job in Stromness at James Wilson, Orkney Ltd, a cash and carry wholesaler. With having the two jobs, my time, energy was getting used up in a positive way.

For poor Joanne, her days were long, and with having no real friends or family, then she slipped into a depression, and I did not help in the matter. For me, my life was looking great, back in my old turf, working two jobs, back playing football for Stromness, which felt like a dream come true. At the age of 28 years old, feeling as fit as ever, it was fantastic to be back playing at the Market Green again. The old nature was coming to the surface too, after a game or when the weekends would come, I would head out for a few beers etc.

Writing this makes me feel like, "what a plonker you were Ricky Bain", oh man …selfish or what! Joanne and I had too many blazing rows and one night I came home, and she threw a cup at me, which smashed against the wall. Yep, life was tough, especially on Joanne.

The blessing though was that we were around my former Boy`s Brigade leader, he and his wife were so good to us, making sure Joanne was not alone, and they made us welcome at their home. This became a safe place for Joanne. They encouraged us to attend Kirkwall Baptist Church, so we started to

WILL YOUR ANCHOR HOLD

go every Sunday, doing this was a God send and for Joanne you could sense her faith life coming alive again, and this made me happy. My thoughts were "Happy wife, Happy life" lol

Joanne and I were still at each other, being just married, and in reality, getting to know one another, then things did not look good for our future together. Joanne`s brother came up for a few days, he was getting over a relationship and wanting some time out, so up to Orkney he came. What do most guys do to get over life`s struggles, yes we go to the pub, and that's what me and her brother did for the next few nights; we played pool, got drunk and I sang on the local karaoke circuit, same songs in different bars.

On one of these nights, I was having a laugh at the bar with some girls, and out of the corner of my wife I saw Joanne heading right towards me. She was so upset, and I could see that I should get home, or this could be the end. After Joanne`s brother left things did calm down, and amazingly Joanne gave her life back to the Lord, she was a good place spiritually. Also, she found a part time role, looking after the dad of the BB leader, so the extra cash was very helpful. For me, I was happy to go to church and I did enjoy some of the sermons, but there was no active faith in my heart, and I was content to keep Joanne happy.

WILL YOUR ANCHOR HOLD

One thing that still bugs me though is the fact that I was selected to go to the Orkney inter county trials, and I was playing some of the best football of my life, so chuffed to be selected. However back then it was frowned upon if a church goer would play football on a Sunday, and I was fuming with this attitude. So, I remember watching the County players training on the Market Green from a distance, my heart sank and I thought 'if this is faith then forget it'.

The final nail in the coffin for the Orkney venture was one day while at work, a guy who was a friend to me, but had his issues in life, had come into our home in Orkney verbally abused Joanne and went nuts in the house. Joanne had called me, and I quickly came home to find Joanne shaking, crying and scared. You know, looking back I should have punched his lights out, there was no excuse for his behaviour that day. Even then I had a forgiving heart, but should have stood up as a man.

The baby was due soon, so both Joanne and I were so excited for the big day, Joanne was remarkable, resilient and one brave lady. We did have a dog called Monty and a hamster named Dougall, these two did help Joanne, well apart from cleaning the hamster cage. The day that our baby appeared, I was working at Wilsons and excited about the football match that night, when my best friend appeared to say that Joanne's water had broken, with baby on its way.

WILL YOUR ANCHOR HOLD

We arrived at the Balfour hospital, and as they have always done, the care for Joanne was first class from our arrival. Joanne`s mum had travelled up from Tain, and she was allowed into the labour ward, along with a couple of student nurses. Imagine that happening these days, not a chance. I think it was twenty seven hours labour for Joanne, and during this she was having severe contractions, one of these she grabbed my hand very tightly, and I pulled a face in pain , she said in a firm voice " What is wrong with you?" You see I had a huge cut on my thumb, and she had grabbed my hand so hard that my thumb was sore. She replied, "get a grip Ricky!", I didn't say a word back to her!

Katie was born on the 13th May 1996, we had a beautiful baby girl, what a joy I felt in my heart, me a father, wow what a feeling and now what a responsibility too.

Joanne was back home with Katie within a couple of days, she had been well looked after by all the wonderful staff in the Balfour Hospital. Joanne and I had a deep, sensible chat over the next couple of days, and deep down I knew that we had to leave to keep our marriage together.

Joanne, as you read this book and mainly this chapter, I am sorry for putting you through so much in the early stages of our marriage. I thank God for you, for who are, and I love you more today than yesterday, but less than tomorrow.

WILL YOUR ANCHOR HOLD

CHAPTER 9 - THE BATTLE

Now heading back to Aberdeen, I got a job in Portlethen through the agency Joanne used to work for. The job was with an oil company called Cameron, they were Cooper Cameron back in 1998. The job was a storeman, or nowadays 'storeperson', officially a Monday – Friday role, but the overtime was unlimited, so I was working six days a week with Sundays off, and my weekly wage was huge!

We were now back at my flat, we had rented this out while away in Orkney, it was only a one bedroom, so knew we would not be there for long. I loved being a dad, and there was nothing better than coming home to a beautiful wife and now baby Katie was here. Katie had a night-time routine, bath then off to bed, Joanne was a natural mum and she made motherhood look easy, what a gift. Our favourite time for me was lying on the bed with Katie with the lights out and watching the night-time baby mobile, think they were called Fisher-price Butterfly3- in-1 dreams projection mobile. For the first time, I felt the change from immaturity to fatherhood, knowing I had a huge responsibility with a wife and baby to look after. These early days of a family of three were good times, Joanne was delighted to be a young mother, and an amazing home-maker too. After a hard day at work, I knew coming home was a blessing, and was thankful that home was a happy place.

WILL YOUR ANCHOR HOLD

With work now a focus and earning good money, my football days had ended. I did go back to Junior football with Banchory St Ternan's, but this was a short stay, and with the combination of what is called 'chocolate ankles' and less time to go to training, I made the decision to hang up the boots from 11 a-side football.

With leaving Orkney, my mentor the BB leader had made connections with a church in Sheddocksley , so we started to go to this church every Sunday. We were made so welcome, and I enjoyed going to this church, the message each week was one of the highlights of my week and I looked forward to what was said.

God was moving in my heart, and I knew my life was about to change. Each Sunday service there was always the shout out to shake a hand a say hello to someone, a way of connecting in the church. On one occasion, I was sitting behind a guy who had preached a couple of weeks previous, his message had made an impression on me, he shared from the bible, along with his life story, a winning formula.

Well on this particular morning when the shout went out to shake a hand and say hello, I got more than I bargained for, the guy in front on me turned around, shook my hand and said "How are you with God?!". Wow what a statement, and what he said penetrated my heart and my mind too. It is said that many people can say the same message, but it's the delivery that counts. Well, what this guy said to me I received it well, his delivery was perfect for my personality. It was man to man, and because I had heard his testimony just a couple of weeks back, I didn't think "who do you think you are?", my inner spirit man took this comment on the chin.

One thing about me is I don't do flaky or weird, and what happened that day was neither of these, it was like a dart hitting the bullseye. A big thankyou to this guy, he was obedient to the Holy Spirit that day, and believe me he`s impacted many into the Kingdom by being brave, not caring what reaction he got. When God is chasing after you, it is impossible to get away, but like the gentleman he is, he will not force himself on you. Life is all about choices, so going forward the biggest decision I was about to make was about to happen.

In the church we started to make friends, even though the mischievous side of me was never far away, and Joanne was always a bit nervous when I was surrounded by church folks. We were in the church, Katie was just starting to walk, she had made it up onto one of the church tables, and did a wee baby dance, my mind went into overdrive. I said "Yep, that`s how I met Joanne, she was a table top dancer". Well you should have seen the look of their faces, some with shock, others with a sly grin and many chuckling away to themselves. Of course Joanne was shaking her head, denying it all. I did it

WILL YOUR ANCHOR HOLD

just to see that these folks are not actually too bad and do have a sense of humour.

One couple asked us around on many a Sunday for food, and I liked the guy, he was down to earth, easy to chat too and was passionate about his faith. Over the next few weeks, we had built up a good friendship and then one Sunday he asked me if I wanted to go to an evening at Gerrard Street church. I asked him what it was all about, and he shared it was just a night where many Christian people from all over the city where coming together for a night of praise and worship.

There is a battle for a soul, between good and evil, so with this church get together being on the Thursday evening, I got to feel the unseen battle taking place. From the Monday to Thursday my mood was not good, feeling unsettled too. Joanne could sense what was happening to me, like the lovely lady she is, she backed off, was full of grace and prayed for her husband. When I came home from work on the Thursday night, I was saying to Joanne "I am not going, no chance", going off on a rant. Joanne never said a thing, just giving me the space to go off on one. Soon the phone rang, it was my friend to give me a lift to church, my reply was " Yes no probs see you soon, looking forward to it". You should have seen Joanne`s face, what a picture it was, a lovely picture though lol.

WILL YOUR ANCHOR HOLD

Before I knew it, I was in my friend's car heading to Gerrard Street Church. God has a sense of humour, and He is full of grace, even through bad attitudes like mine that night. There was a large gathering inside the church, a big worship band was in place, a good atmosphere in the building. As the night went on, there were many worship songs and testimonies spoken from folks from various backgrounds. Near the end of the night there was a cry for the Holy Spirit to come down, and this is where my mind started to wonder. I could see many people crying, others on their backs, people praying and singing out in what is called 'tongues'. I was spooked to be honest, and looking for a sharp exit, when my friend said to me "Ricky, are you ready to give your life to the Lord", and you know what, amongst all the chaos around me, I said a simple prayer to ask Jesus into my heart.

The prayer seemed easy to say, suffice to say the battle for my soul had indeed taken a long time. I guess getting over my pride is something that had held me back from confessing with my mouth that Jesus is my Lord and Saviour. God knows the heart and with opening my heart up to Jesus in spirit and truth, my born-again journey began in October 1998.

Life was full on, with work, family, church and Joanne, Katie and I were a tight unit. Yes being a Dad had changed me beyond all the expectations of what I had ever envisioned.

WILL YOUR ANCHOR HOLD

I started work at 7am, so up at 6am to head to work, which was a forty minutes' drive, so plenty of time to pray in the car as I headed to work. I finished work usually around 16:30, sometimes later if required. A long day in the workplace, and it was a busy company, where I could have worked twelve hour days, seven days a week. However six days a week was long enough, family time was vital to me.

The guys at my workplace knew that I was a Christian, and I got the usual banter, most of my work colleagues were okay with it, but the majority with the attitude, "If it works for you, then all the best, don't bother me though". With my newfound faith in Jesus, I was excited to share it with everyone, and it didn't bother getting stick or labelled a Bible Basher, sometimes worse too.

The church invested in everyone, and with me being a new believer I was encouraged to continue the one to one book with my friend who taken me to Gerrard Street. I was keen to know more and made sure I made time to do the weekly study with my friend, usually every Thursday evening. From the off, I knew that to grow in my faith, I had to make an effort, not relying on someone else to make sure my relationship with God was in a good place. Faith was 24/7 for me, and wherever I went, I knew Jesus was with me, whether in church, at home, in the workplace or anywhere in fact. God is not confined to a building, I will share more about this later on,

WILL YOUR ANCHOR HOLD

something I want to express more of, as I believe it's vital that God is not put in a box.

The journey Joanne and I have taken is not dull or boring, and when Katie was still toddling around, Joanne had confirmed that baby number two was its way, due in June 1999. I felt so excited, although we also knew that we would need a bigger house. We had put our flat on the market, and also, we had seen a bigger house not too far from where we stayed. Before we knew it we had moved to a lovely house in Auchmill Terrace. Our new home had two bedrooms, the rooms were bigger too, and there was a nice size garden at the back of the house. With Joanne being pregnant, and looking after Katie, this was a full time job for her. We didn't really have any help, with Joanne's parents up in Tain, and my Dad staying with my middle brother, which was a full time vocation for Dad.

The routine was work, work, family, church with the odd day out at the weekend. Thankfully Joanne's pregnancy was going well, with no adverse effect on her wellbeing. Joanne was a natural mother, bonding with Katie. Joanne made my life easy, always food on the table and coming home to a wonderful home maker was a blessing. I didn't appreciate it at the time, that's for sure.

My faith journey was going well, Joanne and I had made the decision to be baptised, by full immersion,

WILL YOUR ANCHOR HOLD

submerged in water. We did this a nice warm baptism tank, not in the river or sea.

Joanne was heavily pregnant, so care was needed as she was baptised, and doing it at the same service was a beautiful occasion.

Why get baptised by full immersion you may ask?

Baptism is a symbolic act. It symbolizes death, burial, and resurrection. And can only be done by immersion. Going under the water represents the death and burial of Jesus Christ, but it also represents the death of our natural selves. Being brought up again from the water is symbolic of the resurrection of Jesus Christ and represents being reborn as his covenant disciples. Jesus was baptised in water, so as a follower of Christ we were following in his footsteps.

Church life was going well, and Joanne and I were in a happy place, our routine was a good one, and being parents suited us both. As you know life is full of ups and downs, and what was about to happen was a game changer.

A few weeks before baby number two was due, I received a horrible phone call at work from Joanne at work to say that my middle brother was missing! The date was 1st May 1999, the May day holiday weekend, Joanne called me mid-morning on the Saturday. Yes, I was in racking up the overtime, for very good money. After the phone call, my mind was beginning to wander to worst case scenarios, is my brother dead or has he had an accident? It was so unlike him go out at the weekend, where is he?

I left work to head over to see Dad, I knew he would be in a state, and when I arrived at his friend's house, he was chain smoking and obviously worried about where is son was. I did my best to help him, saying "Dad, it's okay, he will turn up!" When I returned home to Joanne, and as the day progressed into the evening, I did start to fear the worst.

The phone rang early evening, it was my Dad's friend to say that a body was found in the harbour, and the Police believe that it is my brother. Hearing these words, "it looks like your brother's body has been found in the harbour", can't be true, "it cannot be him" was what was going through my head, no way can this be happening to my brother. The tears started to flow, and the emotions kicked in, and yes I did shout at God, boy was I angry. I felt justified too to shout at God "Why Lord? My brother doesn't deserve this, my Dad will be heartbroken".

Joanne left me to it, she knew that if she said anything then I would have shouted at her too, so I went outside to the garden, to calm down, to gather my thoughts and try to rationalise what was happening. The grief was unbearable, no one will understand unless you go through the loss of a family member, no book or no procedure or

WILL YOUR ANCHOR HOLD

instruction can prepare you for the anguish, heartbreak and devastation that I was feeling.

Dad was my first thought, and I knew that getting to him was now the priority, my middle brother and Dad had an amazing, relationship, a bond that was now broken. I knew he was at his friend`s house, which was just five minutes away in the car, so I sped to the house. Seeing him totally heart broken in the chair, with a cigarette in his hand, is something that will never leave me, no parent should have to go through the death of a child, it is not the natural order.

With my older brother staying in Orkney, then quickly I realised that I would have to be strong for my Dad, he was devastated, just numb to what had happened. This is where my faith in the Lord started to kick in, I could feel his closeness, there was an army of people praying : Joanne had rallied the church to pray, and yes prayer works, although maybe not in the way we think it should. God was my rock throughout the loss of my brother, Joanne as always giving out her heart to make sure life was as easy as possible for me in the days ahead.

With my brother having drowned, I now was called to go to the Police station to identify the body, not something I was wanting to do, but knew that my Dad did not have the heart or strength to do this. At the Police station with my dad and my father In-law, who came to support me, something he would do all

WILL YOUR ANCHOR HOLD

the time going forward. Deep down I was still hoping, praying that my brother was still alive, this changed when the Police officer took in my brother's watch, ring, necklace in a clear bag, the reality that he was gone was hitting home big style. Dad was now inconsolable; he too was still holding out that this was all a horrible dream. Dad was not up for going down to identify the body, I knew this and was ready to do what was required. My Father in-law was right behind me as I walked down to underneath the Police station to confirm that the body was my brother. As we approached the window with a curtain, the officer explained that the curtain would be drawn back and that the body would look swollen due to the water intake. The curtain was drawn back and there was my brother, lying on the table, yes his body was swollen, but it was him. The tears started to flow, then a hand came on my shoulder to comfort me, it was my father in-law, a good man with a huge heart.

For weeks after his death, my dad would take the route down at the beach in Aberdeen, his own way of dealing with the loss, something he would never recover from. Dad felt guilty that he had let my brother become more independent, he blamed himself for my brother's death. Nothing could be further from the truth, Dad had been dedicated to all the family and especially to my brother. The way Dad gave up so much to look after him was love being played out, my Dad never gave up on his

WILL YOUR ANCHOR HOLD

middle son…maybe society at the time didn't have a place for him, his Dad certainly did. For me, the loss of a brother who always made me smile was tough, we were very close, more so the years when I was at home. With my brother having nearly drowned in Kirkwall as a boy, he hated having water over his head. Which meant I had to wash his hair in the bathroom sink, reassuring him that all is okay, and the water will not hurt him.

Yet, he drowned in Aberdeen harbour, and to this day we have no idea how he ended up in the water. I am thankful that his body was recovered though, his body was seen in the water by someone who worked on the ferry from Orkney. We could have had a situation of a missing person who would never return, so we are very thankful that his body was found.

I received many sympathy cards, and there was lots of heartfelt words to comfort me, especially the ones with scripture on them and these versus from Proverbs 3 v 5-6 "Trust in the LORD with all your heart and lean not on your own understanding; in all your ways submit to him, and he will make your paths straight".

I did trust the Lord with all my heart, but I did not understand what had happened to my brother, something I still don`t understand, yet I have peace in my heart that one day we will meet again.

WILL YOUR ANCHOR HOLD

Joanne was heavily pregnant when my brother died, so my eyes were on my wife too, she had to look after herself and not get upset. She was remarkable, and life is easier when Joanne is around, she is a fixer, so she made sure the Bain household was looked after.

WILL YOUR ANCHOR HOLD

CHAPTER 10 - THE EVER-GROWING FAMILY

Joanne and I were baptised not long after the death of my brother, so it was such a blessing to have a wonderful celebration of growing in our faith and knowing that we as a family were in a good place, with another baby on the way.

One day a much better phone call at work happened, Joanne was due to give birth to our second child in June 1999, but was two weeks overdue. On the morning of 6th July 1999, I got the call to say that Joanne's waters had broken and that I should head to the hospital as soon as possible. I sped from Portlethen to the maternity ward at Aberdeen Royal Infirmary to be with Joanne, hard to believe that baby number two was on its way, with Katie being just over a year old.

There was a big difference to Katie being born in Orkney and now baby number two on its way in Aberdeen. Kirkwall was more personal due to less babies being born, so Joanne had much more care with more staff available to help. Joanne was now in the Aberdeen labour ward, baby was on its way, and all was well, no issues, but what would I know - being a man.

There was a student nurse from Ireland with Joanne, and she was good fun, the banter we were having was funny, that's how I cope under pressure, with humour. There is a time and a place of course,

WILL YOUR ANCHOR HOLD

Joanne was not amused and made this known, so back off I did. Baby number two appeared, a healthy beautiful girl, and we named her Hannah, which means in the bible 'favour' or 'grace'. It is a biblical name, with Hannah appearing in the Old Testament as the mother of Samuel.

We were now a family of four, and both Joanne and I were the proud parents of Katie and Hannah, two amazing girls who would be close growing up together, with only fourteen months separating them. Joanne again was amazing, motherhood was indeed a gift to her, and she delighted in having her two wee girls at home. The sleepless nights were again upon us, more so for Joanne, she was up through the night, making sure I had enough sleep to hit the work at Portlethen. I was still working six days a week, usually at least nine-hour days, with an ever-growing family,

While working in Portlethen my faith was strong, even though I knew that I was the only believer in the store/workshop/ yard. If there was another Christian in the workplace, then I did not know them, or our paths never crossed. Building friendships or relationship came easy to me, and being a working man, then where I worked fitted my personality and I had common interests with those around me.

Most working men love their sport, especially football, so this I can certainly do, very easily has it happens, I covered all the bases in the workplace for conversations. The male banter through sport was often a stress relief, yet at the same time could be heated too. With me being a blue nose I had to be wary in not going too far with Rangers being the team to beat in the 90`s and early 2000s. There were four guys in the store, and we were busy all the time, the supervisor was a grafter and he expected us to follow his example. He was good to me and respected my faith, he would often ask about the message from the church on the Monday morning. You can tell when a person is intrigued in your faith, they ask the questions without being prompted, for a so-called evangelist this is good.

'Evangelist' was the name or label given to me by other church members, it means a person who seeks to tell others unashamedly about the Christian faith, especially by public preaching. For most people an American television evangelist might come to mind. A TV evangelist I am not, in fact I can be put off by the American TV Evangelist, too much in your face if I am honest, it seems to work in America, but our country is different.

As I shared, I find speaking to people and making friends quite easy, although the word 'evangelist' I don't know is for me? Back then I would not stand up in front of people to share in church or preach a message, not a chance. However chatting one to one in a conversation, this was easy for me and more importantly comfortable. I could bring faith/God into any conversation, whether, sport, work, movies, family or whatever. God gave me the gift of communication to an audience that don't go to church, which is 97% of the population in Scotland, that's a *lot* of people. I don`t like to be labelled, or to label people, so for me, I am just a guy that loves people and I want to get along with them and help them to hopefully know Jesus one day.

Home was my happy place, I loved coming through the front door and seeing Joanne and the girls, they were, and still are, my world. Being a husband and father did suit me, and I grew into these roles, in fact you never stop learning, enjoying the journey is vital. Joanne is an amazing wife, mother, and more, she ticks all the boxes in life, and I am truly blessed to call her my wife. Our home was mainly a happy place, we did have our disagreements, we both wear our hearts on our sleeves, so life could be feisty. They say couples in conflict are either hedgehogs or rhinos, for many couples you get one of each, but for Joanne and I, we are both rhinos!

Katie and Hannah were a delight, both fantastic personalities, and nearly laughing all the time, life was fun for them. Being a family of four was enjoyable, yet Joanne and I knew there would be more kids to come, we both wanted a big family.

Church life was busy, going every Sunday, as well as a midweek group, like a community group. Joanne and I were placed into a wonderful group of people, most were well into their late 60s/early 70s, and looking back, God knew what he was doing by having a young family placed in amongst amazing mature Christians who helped us grow in the Christian faith. I am so thankful to all those who invested into our lives. Many of these people are now home with the Lord, and we are so honoured that they shared their wealth of life experience with us, thank you.

Joanne was on the go 24/7, a woman on a mission, giving out all the time, smiling along the way, she loved her life, and this was evident to all who were in her company. Katie and Hannah were blessed to have Joanne as a mum, they both excelled with having a safe place to grow, with so much love thrown into the equation.

Work had been going well, then I heard that there was going to be redundancies at the company. With me being an agency worker I thought I would be first on the list. Joanne and I, along with our community group, spent much time in prayer, of course asking for favour, but knowing that whatever happens then God is still in control. As the days went past I saw fellow work colleagues losing their jobs, which was heart-breaking to witness, yet still I was safe. My immediate boss told me to keep my head down, they were wanting to keep me, even though I was employed through the agency books.

WILL YOUR ANCHOR HOLD

All good, until one of the staff employees' complained that there was still an agency worker keeping their job and he was being made redundant. The staff employee was correct to complain, an agency worker should not still be in the workplace while the staff members are being made redundant. It was a Friday and I was told to go and see the manager; I knew what was going to happen, he was visibly upset, he actually shed a tear as he told me I had to be released. My immediate supervisor was emotional too, and again showing his softer side, this of course got to me, and I shed a few tears.

Before I left in the afternoon, I wrote 'Jesus loves' on a blank A4 paper, photocopied at least fifty copies, and went around the store putting the copies in storage bins, pallets on the racking. A good way to leave, on good terms and sharing the love of Jesus. Sure, there would have been many copies found weeks, even months after left, many would have been thrown in the bin, but I'll never know this side of heaven of the impact of my 'leaving gift'.

From there I worked at Balmoral for a few months, this was shift work again, which worked for the family, the money was less but we managed okay. With not being skilled or having a degree, life in the workplace can be a struggle, please stick in at school. I shared a lift with a neighbour who also worked at Balmoral, so Joanne was able to have use of the car, which was a bonus to her and the girls. The work was full on and actually quite dangerous,

WILL YOUR ANCHOR HOLD

but I persevered, and thankfully the team of workers on shift were first class, it is so important to have good work mates, helps to get you through the shift.

Again, the guys knew that I was a born-again Christian, and nightshift especially we would have some great conversations or debates during the break times, they were intrigued by my story. "What changed you?" or "Have you always gone to church", were the most asked questions. Another one was, "You don`t look like a Christian", it's amazing how the majority of folks who don't go to church have a perception in what a Christian should look like! From my experience in the blue-collar world, they have this image of a Christian being highly intellectual, more from the professional world and keep themselves to themselves. Why would a guy who is just ordinary, loves sport, has a beer and talks like any other working lad believe in something that seems pretty alien to them?

Building genuine friendship with those around you helps you get the chance to share about faith. Those around us are open to listen to you when they see a genuine person, who looks and sounds like them, yet has a deep faith they don`t know much about. The Balmoral venture was always going to be short one, I applied for staff positions within the oil industry, and thankfully I was offered a full-time staff position at a company called Red Baron, again in Portlethen.

WILL YOUR ANCHOR HOLD

The job position was not the most glamourous, but it was a full-time staff position, and the money was good, working Monday-Friday 08:00 to 16:30 one week and 08:00 to 18:00 the next week, so every second week was on-call. My job was working in the grinding shop, which involved using large grinding machines to grind various down-hole tools that had been welded from the welding shop. A messy, dusty environment so fully-masked all the time, a sweaty place of work. Again, a busy place of work and the days flew past, and I had a good boss who was approachable, this is so important in any workplace.

At home life was good, but a bit of a squeeze in the house, we had a two-bedroom house, so Katie and Hannah were now in bunk beds, and very happy too, they got on great together. Katie loved her milk, "more milk!" would be the shout from the bedroom. Hannah loved her dummy, so supplying milk and making sure Hannah her dummy or 'num num' as she called it, was the way of keeping the peace.

Then one day at work a text from Joanne "Just done a PG test". I read it more than once, my reply was, "hope that's teabags you are talking about lol". I called Joanne, and she confirmed that she was pregnant with child number three. I was not shocked, delighted in fact, only thing was thinking, how do we survive with three kids in a two-bedroom house? Joanne was a happy lady, she adored her kids and was now looking forward to baby number three, and the way Joanne dealt with life was singing around the home, she loved to worship God in song and prayer, that's Joanne at her happiest. A praying wife, that was Joanne to me, I knew she was in prayer at home, and she battled for me many times in prayer, she had my back when I was in a corner, or feeling the heat at work.

Telling family and friends that we were expecting baby number three was fun, its then you get the comments like "Wow, you guys are on a mission", "Amazing, congratulations" , but you couldn't beat my Dad`s reply "You`re like a pair of rabbits!", aye only Dad could have said that.

No matter what was said, even in jest, we were both delighted, our baby was due 4th September 2001, and this pregnancy was not the settled one as the other two had been. Joanne had a car accident,when a guy crashed into the front of our car and then sped off, he had no insurance. Joanne was taken to hospital for a check-up, thankfully mother and child were okay. Then a few weeks before baby number three was due, she feel from the top steps in the garden, right onto her bump, I was just about to leave for work and saw it happen right before my eyes, it was like slow motion, I felt so helpless. Joanne had a nasty gash on her knee, but could not see it, so I reassured her that all was okay. Again we had another hospital visit, baby was okay, mum needed stitches too her knee.

WILL YOUR ANCHOR HOLD

Baby number three was now overdue, and the day that shook the world was September 11th 2001, I was actually watching Sky News when breaking news came through to say a plane had hit the North tower of the World Trade Centre complex in Lower Manhattan. It felt like we were all watching a movie, as a second plane hit the South Tower, a day that would change the world, devastating the USA, with thousands losing their lives. Baby number three came into the world three days after 9/11, she was born 14th September. Rebecca was the hat-trick, now we had three girls in the Bain family. I remember standing holding Rebecca in a room while Joanne was getting checked out after the birth. It felt like I was holding her for a long time, the Maternity ward in Aberdeen is so busy and there was a staff shortage, so we were left longer than we should have been. No adverse effects though and we welcomed Rebecca to the ever-growing Bain family.

As a Dad my heart was to have a boy, having the three girls was a blessing, but I would have loved a boy too. One night I was praying as I was climbing the stairs in our house, and in the Spirit I heard a voice say, 'you will have a boy one day'. This stopped me in my tracks, one of the few occasions I heard an audible voice. As Joanne regained her strength from the birth of Rebecca, we soon realised that having three children was not cheap and we had to have a plan of action going forward. When

WILL YOUR ANCHOR HOLD

Rebecca was about three months old, Joanne went back to work as a carer through the agency she used to work for. I worked through the day, then Joanne would work at least three evenings a week.

Our weekly routine would be that I came home from work, had tea with Joanne and the girls, then Joanne would head out to work. Joanne had created a good routine with Katie and Hannah, they would be bathed and into their pyjamas, bed by the back of 7pm.

It was then Rebecca and I, where I got the chance to bath her and then it was bottle time before she was settled for the night. I was close to Rebecca when she was a baby with Joanne working at nights. With Joanne working agency her time sheets had to be in by a certain day for her to be paid the week later. On one occasion she had forgotten to put her timesheets in on time, meaning no payment for the week later. I was angry and went off on one "How could you forget" I shouted, blah, blah! Joanne saying "it`s okay, God will provide, he never lets us down". I replied "Where is he now, it`s up to us to survive", boy I was furious.

About ten minutes after my rant, Joanne came through to the living room and threw an envelope at me, she said "This is who God is!" An envelope with exactly the same amount as her wage had come through the letter box, Wow! You could say I was lost for words, feeling sheepish and humbled,

WILL YOUR ANCHOR HOLD

Joanne was, and is, full of faith, she never questions God or shouts at Him, unlike me. This would be the first of many miracles we would encounter in our lives, God turns up in His timing, not ours, often last minute, but always faithful.

WILL YOUR ANCHOR HOLD

CHAPTER 11- ON THE MOVE

Living as a family of five was full on and action packed, never a dull moment, and we loved it too, but our home was a bit cramped. The three girls were in one room, we now had two x bunk beds in the bedroom, Joanne and I had moved to the smaller bedroom to utilise the space as best we could.

We had really good friends from church who were now staying in Dunecht, they were renting a lovely house from Dunecht Estates. Joanne and I loved the location, and before long we were enquiring about moving out to Dunecht. They say it`s not what you know but who you know, so our friends from church introduced us to one of the guys who worked in the Estate office, and he was a major influence in our move to Dunecht. We knew that by selling our home and moving to rented accommodation that we would come out of the property market in owning an house. Joanne and I both wanted a big family, and we were excited about the move to a lovely house in Dunecht.

After our house sold in Auchmill Terrace, we were ready for the move to the countryside, the girls excited too. The day of the move to Dunecht was a beautiful day, and I was able to borrow the truck from work to move all our stuff, my boss at work was very helpful in this way. Joanne and I both had good discernment in our faith, moving to Dunecht made sense in our faith journey. We had prayed into

WILL YOUR ANCHOR HOLD

our decision, and our move made sense, we both had peace about it. Life was good in these Dunecht years, the older two girls enjoyed Dunecht Primary school, and Becks was at nursery in Echt, which is roughly three miles from Dunecht.

Work was going well, there had been a position in the workshop for a Workshop Technician. I applied for the position, the boss at work had said I didn't have the right experience, but I persevered, and I got the position. Better pay and not so dirty, now I didn't have to wear a dust mask.

The fitting shop, as it was called, was a tight knit environment, and they knew about my beliefs, so for me coming into their shop was actually a tough process for me. Yet over time I soon grew on them, and became part of the Fitting shop team. We had some great laughs in the workplace, we still got our work done, but laughed along the way. Looking back these were good times, and the work culture was enjoyable, good pay, good atmosphere and good work mates, well most of them. Faith/ Jesus was often chatted about, especially in a one to one opportunity. Many times if I was working on my own a few of the lads would come up and share about the deeper points of life, this gave me a way in to chat about my faith and who Jesus was to me.

One of the welders came up to me one day, and asked if I was interested in joining the Masons. That led me to do some research on Freemasonry, and asked my close contacts about it. When we chatted again about the Masons, I asked if he could tell me more or show their so called Holy Book. He said it`s all done in secret, but I challenged that by saying that I can easily take my Bible in, open it up and look at scripture, being transparent. I asked him why he was in the Masons, he said it helped him in his work journey, saying it would do the same for me. I found out that there were many Masons in the workplace. We agreed to disagree, I told him that Jesus was enough for me.

Where I worked in the Fitting shop, there was a large cork board which had engineering drawings and blueprints for the company procedures and policies. One Monday morning I came into work, there was writing on the top of the board that said the *Right Honourable Rev Rick*, this was written in black marker pen. Out of the corner of my eyes I saw my work colleges watching for my reaction, I burst out laughing, my attitude was, well they obviously see something good me, I was not offended in the slightest.

Red Baron was bought over and became Smith Services, things didn't change too much, but there was more emphasis on health and safety. At Red Baron wearing safety glasses was optional, but under Smith Services they were compulsory, this took a wee while in getting used too. In December 2004 I was asked to go to Kuwait, to help show the guys there the new flagship tool that was called a

WILL YOUR ANCHOR HOLD

Rhino Reamer. I asked my boss how long that I would be away for, since I didn't want to miss Christmas with the family, he assured me that I would be home for Christmas, so I said yes. I flew from Aberdeen to Heathrow airport, then waited for a wee while for the flight to Kuwait. These are times that I get very nervous, out of my comfort zone, the times I do verbally speak to God, I'm sure folks would look at me and think, 'that guy is talking to himself', nope I'm talking to God.

As I approached the check-in desk the lady looked up at me, smiled and said "This is your lucky day, you are being upgraded to First class". I was like "How is that?!", she replied " Sometimes we have spare first class seats, and you are the lucky one today ". In my mind I am thinking, 'you mean blessed not lucky, God is looking after me'. On the plane I was the only person wearing jeans and t-shirt, looking well out of place, a few folks looking over while I am playing with the seat which could move up and down, yep spot the guy that hardly ever travels. There was steak and champagne on offer, I thought, wow!

The three weeks in Kuwait went quickly, I enjoyed my time there, and was well looked after. It is a different way of life, a strict Muslim nation, so no alcohol. The Kuwaitis love their football, I was sitting in a McDonalds, and beside the restaurant was the most 5 a-side football pitches I have ever seen, every pitch being played on, unbelievable.

WILL YOUR ANCHOR HOLD

Where I worked in Kuwait, the workshop was massive, with the majority of the staff coming from India, Sri Lanka or further afield, they were all lovely guys with big hearts. I noticed they were always in before me and still working when I left the workshop, until one day I stayed until they had finished. As we were leaving the premises, here were the guys I was working with, all in their pyjama bottoms brushing their teeth, waving at me as I left in a car. I asked the boss who was driving the car where these guys stayed, he said they sleep in the huts in the yard. I was speechless, thinking this is not right, its slavery, and it is. That night in my cosy accommodation I was praying, 'Lord, this can`t be right, why is our world so unfair', I actually felt guilty about the first class upgrade on the plane, I could only pray for them, hoping a fairer way of life would open up in the months/ years ahead.

No first-class flight on the way back, I certainly didn't grumble though, counting my blessings all the way back to Aberdeen, where I got the greatest welcome ever. Three beautiful girls running towards me shouting "Daddy, Daddy, Daddy". To this day, this amazing welcome brings a huge smile to my face, being a father is the greatest job in the world, and having Joanne as my wife, what a blessed man I was, and still am. Home in time for Christmas too.

Church life was, as always, busy, I was growing in my faith and open to most things that was going on. The only thing I struggled with was the length of a

WILL YOUR ANCHOR HOLD

church service, especially when I thought all was done and someone would stand up to share at the end of the service. One guy in particular would stand up at the end of a service, he would share a word from God, but mostly he would say " I have a picture that the Holy Spirit has given me", sometimes it would make sense to me, but other times I just thought he was crazy, and this made me switch off when he shared.

Then while at home one day the phone rang and I answered it. Would you believe it, on the phone was this guy, and yes you guessed it, he had a picture to share with me. He said "Ricky, the picture I have for you is that you and your Dad are standing together over a pot of soup. I know it will not make sense to you at this time, but please trust God and don't look at it through natural eyes". As soon as I came off the phone I just thought, this guy is totally of his head, what on earth does a plate of soup have to do with my dad and my Christian Faith, it did not make sense that is for sure. Just a couple of weeks later, my Dad was on the phone saying that since that I did now work in Portlethen, are you up for coming over some soup at lunch time, would you believe that. For the next few years, I would be having lunch, mostly soup with my Dad, this would open up some deep conversations with my father, God is in the details.

WILL YOUR ANCHOR HOLD

Romans 8 v28 – *And we know that in all things God works for the good of those who love him and have been called according to his purpose.*

There was a blip in my relationship with Dad at this time though… one day he had gone past to see Joanne, and went off on one. Dad was a scary man when angry, but with Joanne on her own, feeling vulnerable, she was deeply upset when I arrived home. I was fuming and went around to Dad's house to have it out with him. He didn't say much when I confronted him, we didn't speak for about two weeks. Dad was stubborn and would not give in or say sorry, I prayed about the situation and felt led to write a letter to him. I made myself vulnerable in the letter, but also reminded him that I would not tolerate his behaviour towards Joanne. He did phone me a few days later, with no mention of the letter. I asked him if he had received it, and he said yes, and then changed the subject. The letter I wrote, I had finished it off with saying *Love from Ricky*, brave yet from the heart. Looking back, I now know that my Dad was hurting, with losing my brother and his wife (mum) within a short space. No excuses for the way he treated Joanne though, he was out of order.

Okay, we already have the big family with the three girls, now Joanne is expecting baby number four. Again mostly people celebrated with Joanne and I about the news, there were a few concerned, how they going to manage with four kids etc. The way I found out about baby number four was that Joanne

WILL YOUR ANCHOR HOLD

felt sick with the smell of washing up powder, she did a pregnancy test and it was positive. We kept it quiet until Christmas time that year, we were up North staying in a magnificent big house near Golspie. We had Joanne's mum to thank for getting the house, the perks of working for Lord Strathnaver, Joanne's mum got a favourable price for booking the house for a few days. When Joanne was in the huge kitchen, her mother opened the oven, and Joanne felt really sick from the smell of venison, and her mother clicked right away that Joanne was pregnant again. We had a few Christmas times up in these big hunting lodges, brilliant fun and always tucked away in the happy memory bank.

Baby number four was due in August 2005, and we were delighted and excited that our dream of having a big family was being fulfilled. Both Joanne and I were thriving in parenthood, and for me as an individual, being a Dad was a perfect fit, I loved it. In 2005 Katie was now seven, Hannah was six and Rebecca was four years old, so yes, we did have our hands full. I can honestly say that Joanne was, and still is the wonderful mother, who made everything look easy. Our children thrived in the homely environment she created, they were planted in an amazing family, I'm so thankful for who I married. Faith was key to our happy family, Joanne and I were both communicators and found talking to one

WILL YOUR ANCHOR HOLD

another about anything was easy, and yes, we spoke our minds too.

Joanne`s pregnancy with baby number four was good, and again she had a beautiful glow to her during the pregnancy, and she loved the experience. Joanne was in the maternity with baby no four, and all seemed to be going well during birth. Suddenly I realised there was a panic, and more nurses appeared, and then this Doctor appeared, he looked at me and said "all will be okay", and he kept talking with Joanne to keep her awake. In this time I had quickly called a christian brother, and told him to get the church to pray, I was worried that I was about to lose my beautiful wife. Joanne was losing too much blood and her blood pressure was very low. Thank the Lord for this wonderful Doctor, who took over the birth of baby number four and before I knew it baby was born, and Joanne was okay, what a worry though. Baby number four was another girl, and we named her Rachel, we now had four gorgeous daughters, and yes, I was now surrounded by females.

Joanne recovered quickly, she was back on her feet in no time. She had to be, we didn't have any family close by to help, and my dad was on his own and getting older.

We were both very busy, I was working long hours and Joanne had the four girls and had started up a childcare business. As you can imagine her life was manic, yet she made it all look so easy and natural. We made sure that at the weekends, it was all about family time; going to the swimming pool, the park or out on the bikes. Where we stayed was such a blessing, right across the road from our house was the entrance to Dunecht estate, and through those gates was paradise, a place where our kids created memories that will last their lifetimes. Our family came first, and this has been our value for having a happy experience in raising our children, we always put them first, giving them our time, love and input.

One of my fondest memories in staying in Dunecht was when Joanne`s Dad knocked at the door on Christmas day dressed as Santa Claus. The girls were screaming with delight, and I am sure they will say that this was one of their best ever Christmas days. Joanne`s dad and mum are wonderful grandparents, full of fun and have an amazing relationship with all their grandchildren.

Work was going well, I was now an established technician, enjoying learning all the aspects in the tools department. My other venture at work was to assist the guy who put on the explosives show for clients. He basically made homemade bombs out of wine bottles bottoms, sugar, petrol, plastic explosives. The explosive expert was an ex SBS man, SBS meaning 'Special Boat Squad'. He had a story or two to share, and he was excellent at his job, a gifted communicator too. I enjoyed helping to set up all these demonstrations, and got to detonate

WILL YOUR ANCHOR HOLD

a few homemade bombs, so watch yourself, I am armed and dangerous!

I did make a fool of myself when down in Hull, we were down to put on a demonstration to the Humberside Police. To my shame we had a meal with all the top brass of the Police in a posh hotel the night before, all expenses paid, unlimited drink too, and I had one too many, and got a bit drunk. Yep, we can call ourselves Christians, but we know that on the journey there are still bumps on the road, and this night was an embarrassing one. Like I shared, being totally transparent, we all make mistakes and I will still make mistakes going forward.

In sharing faith in the workplace, there were two guys in particular who were interested in my faith journey. One guy took away my daily reading book and digested it, and was challenged by the daily readings, he really admired people of faith. Now listen to this one, the other guy was always up for a chat in the deeper things in life. One day he came up to me and said "Ricky, do you believe in angels?", I said "Yes". He went on to say that one night in Crown Street in Aberdeen on a beautiful night, when the stars were shining brightly in the sky, he felt something was watching him, and he looked up into the sky, on top of a church spire he saw what he could only describe as an angel. He shared to me that he had never told anyone before due to fear of being ridiculed, but I did believe his story. Just a couple of weeks before there had been a book sale in church, there was a book written by Billy Graham called *Angels*, I bought it for 50p, a bargain. Billy Graham had encountered a few angels, and his description of an angel was exactly the same description that my work mate had shared. Angels can appear in human form too, I will share about this in another chapter.

Out of the blue a previous work boss got in touch with me to say there was a job going in Westhill, which was only six miles from Dunecht, now this was something to look at. Joanne and I spoke about it, and prayed for direction. I went for a chat with my previous boss, had a look around the workshop and liked the look of the place. What swung it for me was the fact they were working a shift pattern of four days on, four days off, this was very appealing with a wage that was roughly the same, but less travel back and for, so less money on fuel.

Here we were, a family of six, Joanne and I doing our best as parents, loving life in the countryside, but on our journey nothing stays the same for long.

WILL YOUR ANCHOR HOLD

CHAPTER 12- A SEASON OF GROWTH

Starting my new job in February 2006 was exciting, now only ten minutes at most away in the car. Working four days on, four days off, I knew this would be a huge benefit for family life. The first day is always the hardest, with having to meet new people and having to make yourself vulnerable in a new environment. Thankfully the guys at SPS made me feel welcome, and I was comfortable in being in a workshop environment. I was confident from day one that working in Westhill would be a blessing in every way.

The shift team I was allocated was named the A team, the other team was B team, there were four technicians on each shift, and the guys were all experienced in either workshop skills or life skills. My shift supervisor was a good man, he was a natural leader and had really good knowledge of all the tools in the workshop. The other two lads were roughly the same age as me, and they were both 'first class loons' as they say in Aberdeen. Over the weeks we became close friends and I often got a lift to work from probably my closest friend at work, so this freed up our car for Joanne, a win- win for the family.

In 2006, Katie was eight, Hannah seven, Rebecca five and Rachel going to be one in August, we were growing on all fronts; family, work and in our faith.

WILL YOUR ANCHOR HOLD

At church I was involved with the Alpha Course, which is an evangelistic course which seeks to introduce the basics of the Christian faith through a series of questions and discussions. Outreach in church was my gifting, and my heart was for people to know more about Jesus. I found it easy in sharing my faith in an understandable way. I remember when I first became a Christian, I was up for going 'out into the world' as the church puts it, but quickly found out that the majority of Christians in the church building are uncomfortable outside the building, they obviously feel safe behind the four walls. This became evident when I was working with the Youth, along with the Youth worker, who had mentioned that they were going to hand out flyers to the local community, and I thought everyone would be up for going to door to door with the flyers, boy was I wrong, I did it by myself. On the evening, I had a handful of flyers, and before I knew it, I was outside in the dark on a cold night, on my own, no one else came with me!.

Outreach is still an issue with the churches, they are up for asking folks along to church, but they do not feel comfortable in going out into the world, yet the Bible says in Mark 16 v15- "He said to them, "Go into all the world and preach the gospel to all creation".

Anyway, that was back then, so I just went along with it, and helped with the Alpha team in the church. Since I had been open with my faith at

WILL YOUR ANCHOR HOLD

work, my Supervisor and friend came along to an Alpha course. The first night of an Alpha course is relaxed and informal, the food is delicious and it is very much an intro to the course and to one another. The lads from work arrived and all the food was laid out on the kitchen top, my friend burnt his finger on the hot dish and shouted out a swear word, I could not stop laughing, it was hilarious, you should have seen the reaction from a few of the people, they didn't know where to look, I still laugh to myself when I think about it.

They both completed the Alpha Course but did not attend the Holy Spirit day away due to being on shift at work, the Supervisor never made a commitment, but my friend gave his life to the Lord. He got baptised in church too, and he came to church for a few weeks after his baptism. Unfortunately his wife was not for him going to church, and he stopped going so as not to create an issue at home. Every now and then we still keep in touch, he reads a daily reading and prays, but is not associated with any church. He did try his local church, but because of his previous history in being quite a lad (as they say), he was not made welcome in the local church. Someone close to him said "What are you doing here", and I have to say I loved his reply " I am here to worship the Lord, just like the rest of you sinners", brilliant response, and sure it would have humbled that person.

WILL YOUR ANCHOR HOLD

Unfortunately, Christians in the church have let themselves and the Lord down by their actions in the building. I asked another friend to come to church, he had the confidence to go into the building before I arrived, and he just sat on a seat. When I arrived at church, there was lady hovering around, not communicating or making him feel welcome, nope the reason she was hovering was because my friend had sat on her usual seat, the one she always has, that's what she told me when I said "What`s the problem?". My friend moved seats, apologised to the lady, even thought he had nothing to apologise about. I was actually embarrassed about it all, the lady was actually rude to us both, she suffered from spiritual tunnel vision, only seeing through her own eyes. Sadly, my friend never came back to church, and my heart has been heartbroken on the many occasions I have taken friends to church and all have not comeback. I've just got to trust Jesus that he has their lives in his hands.

The biggest joy in my life in church was that Joanne was now part of the worship team, I loved to see her doing worship, she is a worshipper and God radiates from her when she is lost in worship on the worship stage. The kids loved church, the various children`s group from toddlers through to the Youth group was a huge plus at the church, and they had brilliant leaders who gave up their time and energy to help all the children grow in their faith.

WILL YOUR ANCHOR HOLD

On the home front, we were again out-growing the house in Dunecht : Joanne and I had our own bedroom, Rachel was now in a bedroom, Katie, Hannah and Becks were in a bedroom together, sleeping in a triple bunk bed, Hannah was the one who got the bed at the bottom, which is basically a pull out mattress, and with Hannah`s beautiful nature, she embraced it, no complaints.

I have so many wonderful memories from staying in Dunecht, from the estate just across the road to the lovely play park and football pitch just up the road. The years we spent in Dunecht were truly amazing, we were a happy family, a cheerful bunch who loved one another and knew that God had us in his hands.

Joanne was, and still is, a prayer warrior, she spends a lot time in the Bible and listening to worship music, her relationship with Jesus has never wavered in all the years we have been together, so I trust her decisions when she hears from the Lord. One day she shared that there was a bigger house available on Dunecht estate. Now the estate is massive and stretches for miles, so my first question to her was, "where about is this house"? It was roughly three miles from where we stayed, closer to Echt, it was up a dirt track from the long straight towards Echt. The night we were shown around the house, I knew in my spirit that Joanne had fallen in love with the house, and the area.

WILL YOUR ANCHOR HOLD

The house was huge, there were four big bedrooms, a massive living room, and big kitchen, two toilets too, so everything that Joanne wanted was now available. There were outbuildings too, plenty of room for a big family, the garden out the front was huge. Joanne and I knew that we both had fallen in love with this amazing house and perfect location to bring up the kids.

There were a couple of other folks interested, but we had first offer on it thanks to the guy we knew that worked on the estate, he was very good to us, and I will be forever grateful to him for helping our family out on the estate. Of course, we accepted the house, and much excitement started with all the girls loving that fact that we were moving to a bigger place, with all the freedom they wanted. My work was good to me and let me have the truck for the weekend to move all our stuff, and I had help from my church friends too, so it did not take us long to move, many hands make light work. It was actually an enjoyable experience, it's not often you can say that while moving to a new house, it is often a stressful time for the family. Joanne being the perfect home-maker was in her element in sorting out all the rooms in our new home.

Within a short time I had started a new job, and now moved into a new home, the whole family were excited, and we quickly settled into our new environment. My good friend from work continued

WILL YOUR ANCHOR HOLD

to help with lifts to work, freeing up Joanne with the car - happy days indeed.

For my own mental health I had started to play 5 a-side in Westhill on a Monday night, this was brilliant for me, giving me downtime and playing the game I have loved since a wee boy. Joanne encouraged me to go, she knew that I needed time out doing what I loved.

Being brave was something that came naturally to me, and often would get me into trouble, being misunderstood was what I believed, because I saw life maybe a bit differently and did not like injustice or unfairness. God was doing something new in me, and while in church I would feel the presence of the Holy Spirit, my heart would start to beat faster, my throat would go dry, and before I knew it, I started to share from the front of the church. I could only share with the way my personality is, with rawness, passion and directness. I am not polished in speech or the delivery, but something always happened when I did what God asked me to do.

One lady said to me "You should look at being a Preacher, you are authentic, real and full of passion", it was very kind of her to share that. I soon realised that I was like marmite, something or someone that people like very much and other people like very strongly, and I was fine with this. A few weeks before I was sharing at the front of the church, the church had a visiting prophet come along; what is a Christian prophet you may ask?

A prophet is a man/woman called by God to be his representative on earth. When a prophet speaks for God, it is as if God were speaking. A prophet is also a special witness for Christ, testifying of his divinity and teaching his gospel. A prophet teaches truth and interprets the word of God. This prophet shared a message at church, then he would call out some individuals to prophesy over them. He called Joanne and I to the front, and it was like God speaking into our lives, he knew everything about us. What he spoke over me was that I was like a cheerleader in the house of God, my first thought about this was me wearing a skirt with pom-poms, not the picture a man wants to see! Then he shared that I would not accept the status quo, which was spot on at this time, I was starting to feel a bit frustrated within the church structure. He also said that there was a much bigger playing field for me, God will have me on the field to make a difference for the Kingdom. And like I shared earlier about being like marmite, he shared that no matter what words come against me, that it does not affect me, like water of a ducks back, which is true. The prophet was first class, and everyone he had a word for was on the button, he was the real deal, a man of God with a gift. It was a beautiful experience to get a word from the Lord through a wonderful man of faith. It was such an

WILL YOUR ANCHOR HOLD

encouragement too, Joanne and I were boosted by God's good words spoken over our lives.

On one occasion I shared from the front, it was a dream that God had given me, yet while sharing this with the church it was received like a lead balloon, I could feel it myself as I spoke it out. What I shared was that in my dream I saw many people in high-vis vests going on the streets, helping, praying over those in the street. I believed God was saying 'get out of the building, go to the people, and we will see many come to Christ by being brave'. Unfortunately I didn't get much positive feedback or encouragement, again it comes to the fact that most Christians are uncomfortable outside the four walls. I was the opposite, not comfortable within the four walls.

Not long after this, the Street Pastors movement was pioneered in Aberdeen, and yes you got it, I was part of the original team to hit the streets of Aberdeen. Our role was to voluntarily patrol the streets of the city at night, helping and caring for people in practical ways. With working the four days on, four days off at work, this allowed me to do Street Pastors, also a big thanks to Joanne too, she is such an encourager. I remember my first night, we met in a room at Gilcomston Church on Union Street, that night there were three teams hitting the streets in Aberdeen. I was nervous, this would be a very new experience for me, remember just a few years back I would be leading the pack hitting the pubs, clubs and getting so drunk. Now please hear me out, I am not against youngsters having fun in the city centre, I loved it, but would nearly always go too far and get so drunk that my weekends were a write-off. Now I was sober on a weekend night and seeing a different city centre through sober eyes (not the beer googles) and looking to help people rather than chase the girls for a one-night stand. Yep changed days, a total transformation.

My Street Pastor nights were an amazing experience, 99% good; from helping hand out flip flops, which the Street Pastors have become famous for, all Pastors carried them. This was due to girls wearing high heels, and as their night progressed their feet would get sore, the flip flops were a blessing to the many ladies who have used them. We also gave out bottles of water, first aid treatment and there was a few who we got the privilege to pray for, which we all loved to do. The highlight for me was the night on Street Pastor duty, walking towards Castlegate and there were a group of young lads walking in front of us, when one of the lads ran back to chat with us. He was telling us that he had just come back from America, and that the Christians there were not ashamed of their faith, and most Americans embraced the church. He asked why the Christian voice is so quiet in Scotland, that the Christians in this country seemed ashamed in who they believed in. He didn't have to tell me that,

WILL YOUR ANCHOR HOLD

I think this way to this day, the Christian voice is really non-existent in this day and age, and I am frustrated by this even while I am writing it.

We had a good chat and then he went with his mates, the other two Street Pastors and I headed onwards. Our typical evening was starting at 10pm and often finishing around 4am, yes, a long night on the street.

Back to this night, I was passing a nightclub about 1am and I saw the young guy who had chatted with us earlier that night debating with a bouncer. What had happened was that the lad had left his mobile phone in the club and was trying to get back in, but he was a bit drunk. I had a chat with the bouncer, and he let the lad back in to retrieve his mobile, he came back out and thanked me for the help. It was then I felt the Holy Spirit prompt me to ask him to come to church on Sunday. It was early Saturday morning, so church was another day yet. To my shock he said yes and asked for my mobile number, which I gave him, and true to his word he called me Saturday night asking for directions to the church. He came along to church on the Sunday, he continued to come along and eventually did the Alpha course, giving his life to Jesus, but again after a few months, he stopped coming along to church, which is a shame. We have still kept in touch, and recently I had the absolute privilege of conducting his wedding!

WILL YOUR ANCHOR HOLD

The night that got me spooked while Street Pastoring was what seemed like just another Friday night in the centre of Aberdeen. The usual start at 10am on the streets, again going out in a team of three, it was me and two ladies on this particular evening, they were both good Street Pastors and enjoyable to work with. In everything you do, it is all about who you are working with, the team is everything. It must have been about 11pm, early doors for us on the Friday night, the two ladies I was with were talking with some people, while I stood behind them making sure all was well. We were told that if we are out in a three then one has to step back and 'survey the land', being the eyes and ears in case something might kick off.

I was looking around and sensing the atmosphere in Belmont street, when I had this weird feeling that someone or something was behind me, and when I turned around, right in my face was this guy. He was slightly taller than me, with a bushy black beard, and dark glasses, so I could not see his eyes, but what caught my eye was the strange looking cane in his hand with a silver head on it. Without hesitation he said, "What are you doing out here?", my reply was that I am a Street Pastor, he then said "Do you know who I am?". "How would I know?" that was my reply. Now what he said next put a chill down my spine "I am the devil!". My first thought was that this man was on drugs or just weird, but my spirit was uneasy and have to admit I was a spooked by this guy. He then pointed at his boots which had the word *Diablo* on them, which is Spanish for *devil*. We then were face to face, he said "Man of faith, you have no right to be here". I was lost for words, nothing came out my mouth, and before I knew it, he was gone into the crowd. By now, my mind was racing, what had just happened? 'Give yourself a shake Ricky' was what I was saying to myself. My two colleagues were still chatting away to their group, and I waited until they had finished, but never shared to them what had just happened with me.

I carried on that night as normal, well the best I could have considering what had just happened, giving out water bottles, flip flops etc, chatting, praying with people and just being a positive presence on the streets. We had done the full routine, walking all around the streets of Aberdeen, now at the opposite end of Belmont street, the Union street end, again my two colleagues were chatting with a group. Suddenly out of nowhere this man appeared again, looked like he had come out of Café Drummonds, but I could be wrong. He was right in my face and I was backed onto the building, and I froze as he laid into me verbally, like he was talking to my soul, all about the past and what I had done, it was personal and so accurate. How could he know all this? He was talking about all my womanising, drinking and how bad I had been, and I was speechless. To look at him, there was no

WILL YOUR ANCHOR HOLD

threat in a physical sense, and I could have battered him, but his presence was pure evil, and it scared me.

After the verbal and spiritual onslaught he slowly walked away, scraping the strange looking cane he was carrying on the ground, and laughing away to himself, honestly, it could have been a scene from a horror movie. For me, I was like a boxer on the ropes, hanging on in the fight, when all of a sudden, a guy appeared from around the corner and pulled up his sleeve, there was a tattoo in front of me, he said "This is Hebrew for *Yahweh*(YHWH), God is with you young man", and then he just walked off. I am thinking, what is going on, am I going mad?! I was in a daze, trying to compose myself, and thinking 'nobody will believe what had happened to me tonight', so I did not say a word, either to my two colleagues or to the team when we did our debrief. Looking back it was, without doubt, a supernatural experience.

On the home front we were a busy bunch and Joanne was pregnant with number five child on the way. We were growing as a family and growing in faith, both Joanne and I were on fire for the Lord. Our lives were full on for Jesus and we lived to please him, by being good parents, and working hard for our family. Work was going well, and the four days on, four days off was such a blessing to our lifestyle. The only downside for Joanne was that I had to work a lot of weekends, so she had to keep the kids going over the many weekends I was working. She was a natural mother, and she did not complain, she got on with it without a fuss, making sure the kids were always first. Where we stayed made home life such a blessing for the kids, they had lots of room to explore and enjoy the country life.

I actually really enjoyed working the weekends, which might sound strange to you reading this, but the weekends at work, there was no office staff in, and no management to interfere in the workshop. We had a strong team on shift, and the guys were all hard workers who got the job done. The atmosphere was good, and the tunes blasted out over the workshop. We all loved football, so the banter was flowing over the weekend with the endless matches going on, lots of laughter too, a happy work environment indeed. On a Sunday we would have a full cooked breakfast, with all the team bringing the breakfast variety. It was a big breakfast too - sausage, bacon, egg, square sausage, black pudding, beans, tattie scones, aye the whole shebang, this certainly set us up for the day. In the afternoon we had access to *Super Sunday* on Sky, so would often watch a match, and at these times in the canteen, I often got the chance to share my faith. In a way it was doing church in the workplace.

To be honest, I was struggling with just going to a church building on a Sunday, the way church was done was becoming predictable and I was not enjoying just turning up and what felt like going through the motions. After the service was finished we would got through for a coffee/tea biscuits to chat, no one would chat about the message that was just delivered or share about what God was doing in their lives. The ladies would of course, but the men didn't say anything. I struggled with fact that surely after a brilliant message that there would be a discussion about it, nope never happened and then it was a case of 'see you next Sunday'. This bothered me, because there was no relationships being built up with guys at church, unlike my work, where we did life together and would chat about anything and everything, it was transparent.

My faith was on fire, and my heart was in line with God. I was reading the Word and, most importantly, my prayer life was good. Yet I struggled in the building, the four walls were not my passion, I was more at home on the streets with Street Pastors or even on a football pitch or training ground. Those places gave me opportunities to share a message of hope in Jesus in a language that the ordinary person could understand. My faith was growing even though I was frustrated with the institution that for me only seemed to work for the few ie. those that basically knew nothing but an institution, they knew what they went to every Sunday, yes it was a comfortable setting for them. For those, like the many friends who I had asked along to church, they did not come back, even way back then, my mind was saying, the way we do church in this land does not work for the majority, WHY?

Please hear me out : I am not criticising, this is my story and the journey that God has taken me on. I have a huge heart to reach out to people, and I believe it has to do with my upbringing in Orkney, where I was surrounded by a community spirit, and I was in my element chatting with whoever I met. However what I have realised that even in Orkney there is a divide between the church goers and those who don't go. The church up there has isolated themselves too, by expecting the unchurched to come to them, and not going out into their lives, Christians should be going out into the world, yet we stay behind the four walls. Of course the fuel of our faith is prayer, we have to action that as well to make it happen, building relationship to those we meet on our journey.

Going forward in the book, Joanne`s parents had now moved to Aberdeenshire. They had first moved into a flat near the Golf course in Dunecht estate, this was of course like heaven to my Father in-law - he loves his golf, and is very good at it. He is also a brilliant painter/ decorator, and he made their flat in the estate look magnificent in no time, the only downside for them was having no central heating. I admire them for the length of time they spent in the flat, because this would have been very cold for them, but they persevered over the cold months. They did get a move to a lovely house in Garlogie, a

WILL YOUR ANCHOR HOLD

great location too, although this again would be short term as they were looking for a house to buy in Aberdeen. Again the Father in-law put his decorating skills to use, in fact Dunecht estate benefitted from having two places now beautifully decorated.

I named this chapter *A season of Growth*, and I will complete chapter twelve with the birth of number five child. The girls were attending the Dunecht Primary school disco at the Dunecht Public hall. Joanne, as always, was helping out, even though she was due the next day - 15th March 2008. Near the public hall, our good friends just stayed basically next door, so when Joanne was feeling tired she went for a cup of tea. In the house her waters broke, so I had to take her to hospital in the car.... here we go again to the Maternity at Aberdeen Royal Infirmary, which was like our home from home.

The labour for Joanne was going well and before we knew it, baby number five appeared, "it's a boy!" the midwife shouted. I was delighted, over the moon, but only for a split second, because our boy was born with the cord around his neck, and there was no sign of life. The nurse quickly took him into the room where they had the suction machine to clear his airways. Joanne was shouting at me to follow the nurse, I was panicking and fearing the worst, but in seconds I could hear the loud crying. Joanne and I were both emotional and extremely chuffed to have our family complete, we were now

WILL YOUR ANCHOR HOLD

a family of seven. We went to Bampa and Grannies at Garlogie where the girls were staying and shared the good news. I was thanking God, who promised me a son a few years back, and now the promise came to fruition.

We named our boy Samuel, he did cause Joanne a worry in the early days, when he would not feed properly, thankfully he started to gain weight and all was well with mum and son, we were now a family of growth, seven in number.

CHAPTER 13-FAMILY FIRST

Everything in life both Joanne and I did, we gave it all to our family, they were, and still are, our first priority. We are blessed to have five beautiful children who we have poured our lives into. Joanne has poured herself into her children, and me of course!

Many summer nights when we stayed at Meanecht Farmhouse, I would walk up to the field just above our home, look over the land and pray, giving thanks to God for what He had done for us. We have wonderful memories from Meanecht Farmhouse, what an amazing location.

In the bible, Proverbs 22:6 says "Start children off on the way they should go, and even when they are old they will not turn from it. Even as a young father, I recognised the importance in sharing faith with the kids, making it a lifestyle and not just about attending a building on a Sunday. Joanne and I would make sure we prayed with the children at bed times, helping them see that their parents had an authentic faith, living our best lives for the Lord. Joanne and I are both vocal, and we would say what we were thinking - the kids would often say "were you and mum arguing?" our answer was, "No it's a debate"! Obviously, no parent wants to argue in front of the kids, but this is easier said than done, so we did try and leave our debates for times the kids were not about.

WILL YOUR ANCHOR HOLD

With Samuel on the scene and the weekends I was not working, we had spoken about giving the kids our best. This was time for me to leave the Street Pastors, having five kids, now was the moment to make sure that Dad was available and giving the children my time, because you never get that time back, trust me on this one.

We had started to go to a different church as well, our hearts were to get trained and equipped for the years ahead, even then we knew that one day we would do something different in the Kingdom of God. I remember well the first night I went to the church, it was an evening service, they had a guest speaker who was brilliant. He was putting a challenge out to the way church was done, saying that the men need to feel wanted, inspired and ready to be a warrior for Christ, yes my kind of language. I loved when he shared church should be a place "Where the men are men and the ladies feel safe", this has stayed with me. Church in the UK is more feminine, the ladies feel at home in the church culture.

On an American website *Church for Men* they have this take on the situation:

"Today's church offers the things women crave safety, relationships, nurturing, and close-knit community. Women instinctively understand the unspoken rules of church culture …be nice, sensitive, cooperative, nurturing and verbal… On

WILL YOUR ANCHOR HOLD

the other hand, men need risk, but these things are discouraged in church. Although our official mission is one of adventure, the actual mission of most churches is making people feel safe and secure. Men are born risk-takers, but churchgoers are a cautious bunch. Men are all about doing, but the emphasis in today`s church is on becoming. Sadly, a man who tries to bring adventure, challenge and risk into his congregation is more likely to receive a rebuke than a pat on the back"

For myself, I wholeheartedly agree with all the above, the ratio for church goers in the UK is 3 to 1 in favour of the ladies, and the average age of a church goer in the UK is 61 years old, hardly the place a teenage boy or a young man in his 20s is likely to want to attend. In this church we now attended there was more youth, and a more balance of male to female. I also received encouraging words of prophecy over my life, that I would be game changer in the church culture, a man after God`s own heart.

You see I did often grumble about the way church was done and that there was a lack of men, especially the working-class man. One day, a wise old lady said "Son, rather than grumble about it, be the change". She was 100% correct, so this got me thinking, looking and praying for answers/ideas to be a positive change. The church we were now attending held a morning and evening service, and we did usually go to both, I preferred the evening

WILL YOUR ANCHOR HOLD

service, it was more relaxed and an outreach for those who had come along for the first time. Also, it was shorter too, another plus for me. I have always had ants in my pants, and struggle to sit for a long time, whether in school, work or church, if I sit for too long then I start to fidget, and there are many like me.

Our Sundays were full on, with Joanne being a part of the worship team, and all five of our kids doing the various age groups within the church, from primary to the youth. We took the girls through to youth on a Friday night too, they never missed a week, and Joanne and I took week about to drive them, which was a fifty-mile round trip.

Work was going well, we were busy all the time, with a great team working together, the shifts seemed to fly past, and I loved going to work. MI Swaco had a cycle to work scheme in place, I bought a nice hybrid road bike, which was a bargain though the cycle to work scheme. I started to cycle to Westhill, which was seven miles from the Farmhouse, a fourteen mile round trip. My fitness was great and the cycle home was a wonderful way to de-stress before getting home.

At home, the front garden was massive, I cut this with just a normal sized lawn mower. This would take me a while to cut the grass, yet I found cutting the grass enjoyable, I would often pray while doing it. Our kids were happy, they had lots going on from

WILL YOUR ANCHOR HOLD

swimming, Brownies, Girl Guides and the Youth Group at church. Our house was very noisy, full of laughter and fun, the atmosphere was a good one. Joanne and I were a good team and worked well together, loving our children and each other, giving it all our best.

My four days off were a blast and busy, busy, either doing the nursery or school runs, cutting the grass or cutting up logs for the winter, and going into work for an overtime shift. Back then our work/ life balance was good, Joanne had a part-time job at Tesco Westhill too, she worked a few evenings. This helped us greatly and Joanne enjoyed getting out the house, she has gift with people, meeting new folks came easy to her.

At work I got promotion to Shift Supervisor of the A team, which gave me a decent pay rise, the only downside was my good friend going over to the B team, he was my lift to work as well. From where I came from in the Oil Industry, I was chuffed to become a supervisor in such a short time, and now I had to be a decision maker at work, more pay means more responsibility, and more stress too. Now the work environment was changing, when you are leading people, then you have to put yourself last in the equation to have a happy team, something that I had to learn on the job. What I did realise quickly was that I more a people person than a company man, which put more stress onto my shoulders, because people can sense that too. The majority of the staff at MI Swaco were good, but of course like everything else in life, there are personality clashes and Swaco was no different. I did my best to get on with everyone, but there are always one or two that rub each other up the wrong way.

'Treat people the way you want to be treated', this was the motto that my parents had drilled into me, and it stuck. My temper was a chink in the armour, and if injustice appeared, then my prayer life was kicked into overdrive. There was a guy in the workplace who was a stirrer, and could create problems that were not there in the first place. One day I had enough, and I asked him outside and threatened to punch his lights out. Thankfully I backed down and walked away, shaking with anger though. I felt bad after it, not very Christian, that's for sure, just did not like snakes in the workplace, or what I would call injustice. A couple of weeks later I apologised to the guy, he didn't say much to me, yet I felt better in apologising, it was up to him in how he received my apology.

There were one or two confrontations, there had to be in a fast-paced environment and the pressure was on to get jobs out the door in a short time, thankfully no fisty-cuffs.

One night after work Joanne showed me a house that was up for rent in Alford, a place we both enjoyed visiting. The house looked beautiful, and in a lovely location too, certainly something to pray

WILL YOUR ANCHOR HOLD

about. Before I knew it, we were out viewing the house, and we both fell in love with it. There were others looking at the house, the land lady said we had first priority, and we said yes even though we had no funds to pay the deposit. Now that is faith, we were both excited but scared at the same time. With having the older girls at the Academy, and basically never off the road running the kids all over the countryside, we both felt Alford would be the perfect place to bring up a family. Joanne and I were from smaller communities growing up, from Orkney and Tain, we craved the smaller community lifestyle, and Alford looked to have everything that we craved.

We handed in our notice to Dunecht Estates, who by the way had treated us very well, especially the clerk of works. He had made our stay on the estate first class, and I will forever be thankful of his kindness to all our family. He and his wife had the most amazing murder-mystery parties, I remember the first one Joanne and I were invited too, we got proper invitations in the post, and these described what characters we would be; my role was an American helicopter pilot, a suntanned guy. I took the role seriously and Joanne gave me some self-tan lotion, a strong one may I say. On the night of the murder mystery, everyone looked their parts, impressive turn out too, we all sat around the table, Joanne and I were both the murderers and had to look cool under pressure and deflect everything that came our way. It was brilliant fun, and my American accent was so good that the lady of the house thought I was American, but after a few glasses of red wine my accent changed to Pakistani…. we had so much fun, and we did a couple of more murder mystery nights at their home, wonderful times.

We were due to move to Alford on a Friday in September, I can`t remember the actual date, but it was mid-September. The deposit and first month's rent was due on the Friday, and during the week there was money from various sources appearing into our account, but we were still well short on the night before. Joanne and I prayed on the Thursday evening, and knew that God had never let us down, and if we were to move, then it was his will, our faith was strong and we were not anxious. On Friday morning, the money we required was now in our account, we could move to Alford, there was joy all around. The lads on the A team gave us a hand to move all our stuff to Alford, they were a superb team, and gave up their time to help move a lot of stuff from Dunecht to Alford, happy days.

The day we moved was a beautiful sunny day, perfect for moving house. My dad and Joanne`s dad helped put up the beds and also did the curtain rails, they were both good at DIY, one a joiner and the other a painter, a great combination. Joanne`s mum helped with getting all the kitchen things sorted and putting all the ornaments in place, and with Joanne being a natural homemaker, the house soon looked like home. The only downside about the move to Alford was the distance to my workplace, rather than seven miles, we now stayed nineteen miles from Westhill, nearly a forty mile round trip. We did have two cars, which meant Joanne had a car, it was expensive to run two cars though, but at the time we benefitted from having them.

Work was changing, my immediate boss was moved to a different role, and now a new manger appeared, he was already working in the workshop with the filtration department. Now he was promoted to Workshop Manager, he had all the qualifications, and was ex-military too, so knew how to handle the guys. We got on okay, but it was not the same relationship I had formed with the previous Workshop manager. There was now a change of the guard, and work would never be the same, the new manager was more of a barker and often shouted at the younger staff members; you can take the man out of the army, but you can`t take the army out of the man. Don`t get me wrong, this guy was very good at his job, just a different way in getting results, he was articulate and was on the ball in every area.

The atmosphere in the workplace was changing, we could sense the more personal touch and relaxed work environment beginning to evaporate. There was now more pressure on the teams in the workplace, we also knew that the big blue machine

WILL YOUR ANCHOR HOLD

of Schlumberger were in the process of buying over MI Swaco, meaning more procedures and hoops to jump through to get the work done. Within weeks we had now changed ownership to Schlumberger, still under the MI Swaco banner, but now part of Schlumberger and things for me would never the same.

At church, it was a struggle too, the promises from the leadership for Joanne and I were not happening, the training and equipping over the years was now ready to be launched into where our hearts lay, the village of Alford.

We had moved to Alford in 2011, we both had felt the nudge from the Holy Spirit, and being obedient, moved to Alford. One day Joanne was walking with Rachel and Samuel to Primary school and the Nursery, she felt the Holy Spirit speak to her with the verse Joshua 1:3 "I will give you every place where you set your foot, as I promised Moses". When Joanne shared that verse with me, my heart was stirring and I could sense the call on both our lives, a call to one step out in faith and our lives would be full on for his Kingdom.

Whereas the church that we were attending would only talk about building their church, my heart was fully for the Kingdom, not a building. The warrior in Christ that was in me was not designed to just sit in a building every Sunday - give me the open outdoors anytime, a place where I could build relationships with a world that was lost and not interested in God, or should I say interested in God but not church.

At work I had asked my boss if I could do a survey with the lads in the workshop, asking them 3 questions : Question 1 – Do you believe there is a God? Question 2- Are you an atheist? Question 3- Are you agnostic? They all knew the first two questions, question 3 they didn't know the word agnostic, which the noun meaning is 'a person who believes that nothing is known or can be known of the existence or nature of God'. I interviewed over thirty guys, the majority of them were agnostic, unsure what is out there, four believed there was a God. The positive is that there are not many atheists out there, something to work on.

As you are reading the book, there is a theme throughout the book, from the family in Orkney, Boys Brigade, Football, Friends, Workplace, yes, I have been surrounded by men, although of course with my own family it's mainly girls lol. God has given me a huge heart for the men, as I have explained there is a massive void in the church of men, especially those like me, the less educated working man. No-one can deny this in the UK, look around in the church you go to and see for yourself.

In fact, I remember one service in the church, we were all standing, and the minister said "sit down if you are from Africa", then "sit down if you are from

WILL YOUR ANCHOR HOLD

Eastern Europe", then "sit down if you are a student". There were only a few left standings, the local folks who belonged to Aberdeen, just a handful, this got to me, and I thought why is this the way?

For my own development in preaching the word, the Pastor had asked me to share at the Chinese speaking church. Now before you think I can talk mandarin, unfortunately not. I had to share, then an interpreter would follow me, which was funny due to my accent which was a blend of Orcadian/Aberdonian, hard to follow. This was good for my communication skills and helping me grow in sharing a message, and I developed hugely by preaching at the Chinese church. Believe me when I say my biggest battle was speaking in front of people, and this is where God would start to use me, He gave me the strength.

I had helped reboot the men's group within the church, what a battle it is to get the men together!. There is a saying that women are like butterflies in church, they float about chatting not a problem. Men, well we are totally different, we struggle with face to face conversations, small talk is easy, but please don't ask the deeper questions…

For me, it was easier to just do my own thing, well I was the father of five kids (they filled my life), or could easily play 5 a-side football every night, not a problem, that would be the selfish and easy option.

WILL YOUR ANCHOR HOLD

There was a movement in Aberdeen called 'Men of all Ages', they would have men's breakfasts, and they were well attended, but they certainly were not men of all ages, they might have started out men of all ages, now all I could see was Men of old age.

Feeling lonely was something I never thought I would feel in the church, in these days that is exactly how I was feeling as a Christian man. I would get deeper authentic chats with the guys at work or those I played football with, the reason you might ask, it is because I did life with the guys at work and on the football scene. Most church men just have a quick chat after a Sunday service, and most of the time see the same guys Sunday after Sunday, they did not do life together and many guys were there to keep their wives's happy. The guys at work and the football scene are full of passion, unashamed in who they are, most Christian men I have come across are nice, but no passion for who they say they follow, Jesus Christ.

There was a call on my life, I did recognise it, and anytime a prophetic word was spoken over my life, the call to engage with the men was the main theme running through these words. With growing up outside the church environment and being a working-class guy, I have experienced the frustrations in often feeling invisible or by-passed in a church system that has done the same old for years. I will talk about men and church more in-depth in the chapters ahead, yes there is a lot to share and talk about, not to criticise, but hopefully to be part of a solution.

In the workplace, the management had spoken to me about going offshore, which would mean more money and another plus on my career development. I had shared with Joanne about this option, and she said it was up to me and, as she has always done, would support me. For those of you who really know me, you will know that it takes me a while to make a decision, my mind goes back and forth, I struggle to decide and often ask others for their view point, but it had to come down to me.

One day in the workshop, I was checking a load that was due to go offshore, when this guy appeared, he introduced himself, his nickname was Skippy, from Australia funnily enough. He asked me if I was the guy with the big family and thinking about going offshore, I confirmed who I was. He then shared that he had been working offshore for a long time, usually adhoc, which is not on rotation. Meaning you could be home for a couple of days, get a phone call, so back on the rig again, not the best for family life. He also said that his daughter was now fourteen years old, and he hardly knew her due to being away most of her life, yes the money is very attractive but that relationships with those close to you do suffer. For me, this was a clear instruction in what I should do, I knocked back the offer in going offshore, probably not good for my long-term

WILL YOUR ANCHOR HOLD

career, but certainly the right decision in being a present father to my beautiful children.

Again, my walk with God was consistent, what I mean by this is that my prayer life was good, always read a daily reading and facing the battles of life everyday with God. It is said that when the sun is shining, and life is going well, the mountain top experience, then it`s easy to praise the Lord. The hard times are when we are in the valleys of life, that we can still praise the Lord, these are the times when you have to dig deep into your faith.

With Joanne and I having the five children, the cost of providing for such a big family was always a battle, trying to juggle the bills and get by each month, managing our finances was the only downside to our lives. Don`t get me wrong, I was on a good wage, those of you who are parents know how much it costs to raise children, and we wanted to give them the best life possible. When I shared that I had four girls, then the automatic reply was "Wow, think of the cost of weddings", it was never, "what a blessing" or "love that you have four girls"………., not forgetting Samuel here by the way, just explaining the response I got about having four girls. Joanne would often get asked when out shopping with the five children, "are they all yours?!" She would politely reply, "yes they are all mine". 'Family first' has and will be our priority, Joanne and I will give our children whatever they need and being parents suits us both, we love the

WILL YOUR ANCHOR HOLD

family that God has given us, both blessed beyond measure.

At the church we were attending, we could sense that our time was up, we felt it was a striving, performance-orientated culture, having to do things rather wanting to do it. Our time was coming to an end and we both felt shattered in driving back and forth to what I thought was just attending a building, even then, church for me was about people, this was growing the Kingdom. Nothing is wasted in the Kingdom of God; we both knew that we now needed a place to find our feet again and have a time of rest and recuperation.

My good friend was the Pastor of the first church we attended and invited us back to church to rest, find ourselves again with nothing expected of us, we were delighted to say yes.

At this time I had met a guy in Aberdeen who worked for Christian Vision for Men (CVM), they are a Men`s movement in the UK, and this guy was the Director for CVM Scotland. I loved the vison he shared for Scotland, and before long I had become a coordinator for Aberdeen/shire. The role was to engage with the local churches and create Men`s groups, or if they already had a group, then I was to hopefully sign them up to be part of a Movement of Men under the CVM banner, I thought I would be onto a winner.

WILL YOUR ANCHOR HOLD

One of the reasons I had left the previous church was due to the fact that the Pastor did not believe in that I should be working for CVM, he thought this would take me away from the church. I had said that this would help connect and build the Kingdom, it's not just about a church. He had also said that I had to spend some time on the bench, like an analogy of a football team, basically taking time out. Well I have never enjoyed being on the bench, the substitute in other words, never like it when I was playing football and certainly was not going to accept it now.

The CVM role made huge sense, what they offered was what my heart desired and the call that God had put on life, to get out there and reach a male audience, which I believe the church has not connected with, and had even let them down by the way church is presented.

For me especially, the way our time ended at the church was sad, the Pastor went off on one saying that I had my own agenda. We were quickly taken off all the email lists and he also got the rest of the church to basically disconnect from us. Being honest, this was not a surprise and didn`t affect me, but Joanne struggled with the way it was handled. Our good friend and Pastor from our first church invited us back, and we came to rest, recharge and take a lot of time out have quality family time. Nothing was put on us by the leadership team, and

WILL YOUR ANCHOR HOLD

my friend knew my heart for the Men and was hugely supportive for my role with CVM.

In between the transition from the churches, I had to deal with the death of my Dad, we had only been in Alford for a few months, and Dad had been very supportive with our move to Alford, a place that meant a great deal to him as well. When Dad was a young man, his best man at his wedding was an Alford man, and they had kept the friendship going over the years. When we stayed in Orkney, Aberdeen was our holiday destination every year, and on the way home to Orkney, we would go via Alford and spend a night at my Dad's friend's home, which was a welcoming home and we had good fun with the family. Dad was never a complainer, he was a man to get his head down and get on with life, old school mentality, a worker in every way.

The week leading up to his death, Joanne, me and the kids had gone to see him on the Sunday evening, he was in great form and had fun with the kids, and looking back I'm so chuffed we decided to see him on the Sunday night. The day after on the Monday, I had this sense to phone Dad, he then shared that his back and shoulders were very sore, now this was so unlike Dad, like I said, he never complained. I did advise him to got to the Doctor, but as you will guess, his answer was "no I'll be okay". I was worried though, and shared with Joanne that I would stay in touch and go and see him later in the

WILL YOUR ANCHOR HOLD

week. I called him every day that week, and he was still complaining of the pain, again I said "Go to the Doctor, that is what they are there for", to no avail of course.

Friday evening came along, and I was playing football at Goals in Aberdeen, which is an outside five a side arena. I was playing with the guys from work, always great to have a kick about with the work colleagues. The plan was to play football and then head to Portlethen to see Dad, since Goals was at the Bridge of Dee, so Dad was not too far from there. The football was great, I had a shower then headed to see Dad, I was praying on the way to his house, something didn't feel right. As I arrived at his home, I saw the car in his drive, but all the lights were out, and it was only just after eight o'clock I got out my car and knocked on the front door a few times but no answer, I then rang his landline number, but still no answer, and thought to myself, strange.

When I arrived back in Alford, spoke with Joanne and shared my worries, and she said sleep on it and call first thing in the morning. Called first thing on Saturday morning, no answer, called again ten minutes later and Dad answered the phone, he was in agony. I demanded that he call a Doctor, but again his answer was no, I said I would do it!. I called NHS 24 and explained the situation, they said there was nothing they could do, as the call was not from my dad. At this I was frustrated so jumped in

WILL YOUR ANCHOR HOLD

the car and drove over to Portlethen, again praying on the way, I had felt the Holy Spirit close to me all week. It didn't take me long to arrive in Portlethen, if the police had seen me, then they would have stopped me. Dad's car was outside the house, I approached the front door and could hear the television blaring, he was going deaf and the TV was at full volume, now this gave me hope all was okay. The front door was unlocked and I walked into the living room, where lying on the floor was my Dad, and just by looking at him, he was dead. By the time I had phoned him and driven over to Portlethen, he had passed away. He was lying on his back, eyes wide open, my poor dad was gone, and I suppose I went into automatic pilot, called 999 and asked for an Ambulance. While calling for an Ambulance, my dad's daily devotional book was open, the book was Word for Today by Bob Gass, for that day the headline was *Side by Side*, here I was with my Dad, side by side. The paramedic arrived quickly, he was a motorbike paramedic, he quickly confirmed that Dad was dead, then he noticed the Word for Today booklet and asked if I was a Christian, which I obviously said "Yes". He shared that he too was a Christian and asked if he could pray for me, which was such a blessing, and give me peace in this horrible situation. I still look back and see God's hand over the death of my dad. From the Holy Spirit prompting me to call him every night that week, to going over on the Friday

WILL YOUR ANCHOR HOLD

evening, and finally finding him only after an hour of speaking with dad.

Obviously, I had called Joanne, she phoned her mum, who God bless her, came out to Portlethen straight away to comfort me and make sure I was not alone. Those of you who know me, will know that I am not the best at words and usually say things in the wrong context. I had called Dad`s close friend to tell her that Dad had passed away, but my wording was not gentle or good, so my Mother In-law took the phone from me and calmed the conversation.

A few days passed and my oldest brother came down from Orkney to help organise the funeral, he was devastated of course, and we both shed a lot of tears. On the day we had to meet the funeral director, we were told to bring the suit that Dad was to be cremated in, dad was often wearing a suit and he was such a smartly dressed man. On the way to Portlethen to pick up the suit, we had bought a Jim Reeves CD, the song that was going to be used after the funeral service was called *Welcome to my World*, a beautiful song and a favourite of Dad`s. Well we put the disc on in the car and listened to the song, we both started to cry, this song goes straight to the heart, even to this day, if I hear the song *Welcome to my world*, the tears will flow. We arrived at the funeral director and we both were in the office to chat with the funeral director, now the way I often deal with stress is through humour. We

WILL YOUR ANCHOR HOLD

had used this funeral director twice before with the deaths of my Mum and middle brother, and the director recognised me. When it came down to the cost of the funeral, I said " since we have used you twice before, any chance we can get a deal, say three funerals for the price of two?". My oldest brother couldn't believe what I had said, thankfully the funeral director saw the funny side, even in these tragic circumstances.

There was actually more laughter moments later when the funeral director asked me to get my Dad`s suit, which was in my brother`s car, you see my brother had left his suit in the car too. I saw two suits in front of me, and yes you`ve guessed it, I picked the wrong suit and took it into the funeral director`s office. My brother said "that`s my suit!", well all three of us burst out laughing. The amount of support I received from family, friends and the church were fantastic and way beyond, these are the times when you realise that there is an army of support when the tough times come along.

My faith was strong, Joanne was a rock to me, my soul mate who was by my side throughout this traumatic time. No-one loves like Joanne, a lady with a beautiful heart. Now the family whom I had moved to Aberdeen with in 1986 were all gone, Mum in 1993, brother in 1999 and now Dad in 2012, only my oldest brother and I left from a family of five, life does pass by so quickly. On the day of the funeral, there were two large funeral cars

WILL YOUR ANCHOR HOLD

to collect the family, the three oldest girls were brave and wanted to come along to the crematorium, Katie would have been thirteen, Hannah twelve and Rebecca ten.

There was a huge turnout from the lads from work, which gave me a boost to know that they were there to say goodbye to my dad, and this was a blessing to me. Those closest to me were all in attendance too, which gave me strength to get through the funeral.

What did surprise me was the number of guys from Portlethen golf course who came along to say their goodbyes. Dad loved his golf and he was obviously a popular figure going by the amount of men who turned up. The service was done so well, and one day I hope and pray that I will meet my loved ones on the other side of eternity.

CHAPTER 14 ALFORD

The village of Alford, Aberdeenshire is described as a large village in Aberdeenshire, North East Scotland. It's a place that Joanne, the kids and I had fallen in love with, we thrived staying in Alford. We moved to Alford in September 2011, Dad had passed away in February 2012. I was happy that he had been part of the move, helping us out to make it possible, both financially and practically, he was delighted that we had taken the leap of faith to move to Alford.

For the kids there was just so much for them to do; they stayed in a safe neighbourhood, and had the freedom to explore an amazing village that had a vast landscape to explore. From the little play parks to the beautiful Haughton Park, and the river Don, which was such an appeal to the children in the summer time, we were blessed as a family and thankful to God for directing our path to settle in a wonderful location.

For Joanne and I, our lives were full and we both were so thankful in having five beautiful children. Being able to bring them up in a community that was family orientated, with so many wonderful resources at hand to bring up a family that would embrace everything that Alford had to offer. Joanne loved the house we were now staying in, an excellent modern house that had plenty of room for the big Bain family, we were comfortable in our new surroundings.

At work, my shifts were still four days on, four days off, which I loved, and it was beneficial for family life. I had been asked to think about doing Monday – Friday, to oversee both shifts, a Workshop Supervisor position. When I spoke with Joanne we both felt with the kids getting older and now having the chance of every weekend off that I should take up the offer , and within a couple of weeks I was off the shift pattern and onto the Monday- Friday role. This did take a wee while to get used to, and I did miss the shifts and the long time off, on the plus though was being off every weekend, which Joanne embraced.

The work force had been used to my faith, and over the years I had many conversations with the staff. They respected me as a friend, and now trusted what I had to say to them. In fact, my boss often said that he knew when I was chatting about Jesus, because he could see the passion and my body language was expressive, whereas if chatting about work there was a different posture.

When I became the Workshop Supervisor, I had to attend a meeting with all the upper management, since the head of HR was giving a Powerpoint presentation on the vision of the company. The vision was all the company values, policies and how to treat your staff, he presented it well and was a natural communicator. During his presentation he did swear a couple of times, which did not bother me, it was when he kept using the Lord's name in vain that I felt a check in spirit, and my heart started to beat faster and my throat became dry, which meant the Holy Spirit was prompting me to say something.

With now maturing as a Christian, it's all about the timing of when to share, so I waited until the end of the meeting and all the management had left the meeting room. I then said to the HR manager that I had been bothered by what he had said during the presentation, automatically he replied "was it the swearing?" I shared not at all, I am used to that in the workshop. First of all I told him that I was a Christian, and not easily offended, but he had used the Lord's name in vain on more than one occasion. After saying that, there was a silence, I started to walk out the room, he then shouted "Ricky, thank you for being brave in telling me that I used the Lord's name in vain, will make sure I am fully aware next time, and I am sorry". And that was it, he had apologised and we chatted about a few work issues after that, something I thought could have created a problem was dealt with in the right manner, but so glad that I obeyed the Holy Spirit, not to correct the HR manager, just to make him aware, and possibly think deeper about faith.

Then there was the Christmas message I was asked to share to the whole workplace, now that was

WILL YOUR ANCHOR HOLD

amazing. The lead up was mid-December, my manager had come through to the office to ask if I was up for sharing a Christmas message to the staff, I replied "Yes, delighted to", actually thinking that he was half joking. Well, a week later, in the morning before the company Christmas dinner, my manager appeared in the office to say everyone was ready for the Christmas message, my heart did skip a beat or maybe two. I walked out the office into the workshop and I could not believe it, all the office staff had come through to the workshop, wow there was a lot of people now looking at me. Thankfully the Lord always goes before, and my trust in him that day was full of faith. With not being the tallest, I stood on the big torque machine in the workshop and shared a powerful Christmas message, I think I spoke for over ten minutes. I broke down the Christmas story in a way that those in front of me would grasp. I said the engineering department were like the wise men, the workshop team were like the shepherds, that the story of the birth of Jesus was as relevant today as it had been over two thousand years ago.

With having what we call ball-operated assemblies in the company, they have sleeves inside them that are dormant until a ball is dropped to open up the tool. I said that our hearts are dormant until the Holy Spirit opens up our heart to God, He is the only one that moves our heart. Obviously, I shared much more, but hopefully you get the picture, and

WILL YOUR ANCHOR HOLD

after I shared, I got a huge round of applause. With many of the staff coming up throughout the remainder of the day, even at the Christmas dinner to share how much they enjoyed the explanation of the message, even those who didn't believe admired me for being courageous.

For the majority of time in the workplace, I didn't receive any flak or problems from my work colleagues for my faith, although there was one lad who was after a reaction and if I said something he was against it or looking for a debate, which was not a problem. On my screensaver on the laptop, I would often have a biblical picture or Christian quote which was never an issue, until one day one of the workshop staff said that this particular guy had a Satanic screensaver up and that this was an issue with the other members of staff. The workshop manager was called down to the workshop and told the guy to remove the Satanic image from his computer, his argument was that I was allowed to share about God, the manager was not interested in the debate and shut this guy down. Of course, his argument was that if I could celebrate my God, why can't he celebrate his God? I did offer to diffuse the argument by saying I could change my screensaver, thankfully my manager was on my side.

In Alford our lives were busy, the three older girls did Hip Hop street dancing, which they all loved and were good at, it must be in the genes. Rachel was into her football and actually started off training with the boy`s team, she was a natural football player. Samuel was now in Primary School and was a typical young loon, up to all kinds of mischief, coming home from school with ripped trousers and scuffed shoes, as well as squint glasses due to fighting, much to the annoyance of his Mum. She was now having to deal with a young male, who was totally different from his sisters.

Working the Monday – Friday routine was good for where we all were as a family, usually home by 16:30, I was able to help with all the activities throughout the week, taking the pressure off Joanne.

With Samuel in Primary One, he started with the Donside 2008 football team, and I had volunteered to be head coach, another Dad volunteered to help me out as well. I tell you it's an eye opener trying to coach the Primary One boys, patience being the word, you forget how much they have to learn. Thankfully the guy who helped me out was good fun, and we soon clicked as a coaching team. Training was every Saturday morning, and then the football festivals would be on a Sunday, so quite a commitment for the boys parents and coaches. For me too, I was back playing football with a lot of the dads, which was brilliant fun, and I could still move, dribble and showboat a wee bit too. I loved playing the beautiful game, something I was created to do, no doubt about that.

WILL YOUR ANCHOR HOLD

In my Spirit I knew that as a family the Bains were in the right place, Joanne loved the village, and the kids were thriving in this wonderful village setting, a place where God had placed us, His timing not ours.

We did manage to go away on holiday, a two week adventure to Tenerife. As you can imagine, we had never been abroad as a family together, the kids were extremely excited, but think it was Joanne who was more thrilled, she was over the moon - happy wife, happy life and all that! We flew from Glasgow in August 2012, the flight was okay, apart from the landing, which was very bumpy, lots of screaming from the girls, and from me, but I kept the scream inside since I didn`t want to alarm my children.

The holiday in Tenerife was such a blessing to us, and we will have these wonderful memories for a lifetime. It was two weeks of wall to wall sunshine, with so much fun and laughter. Joanne and I both knew that this was probably a once in a lifetime chance of taking five kids abroad, the cost was huge, but I am delighted that I listened to Joanne because I was more cautious in having to spend a lot of money for two weeks. The holiday was all-inclusive, and from the moment we arrived in Tenerife it was a full on, action packed adventure. From having to get up early to put the towels on the sun loungers, trying to get seven together was nearly impossible, often a four and three lounger combination being the best I could do, the other holiday makers must have thought I was German lol.

There were kids' clubs, so plenty for the kids to do, with Katie, Hannah, Becks growing into beautiful young ladies, as a dad I was protective. Rachel and Samuel were seven and four so we had to watch them at the pool side.

Tenerife has an amazing waterpark called Siam Park, and we visited this a few times, the place was always mobbed. Joanne and I were on the ball looking after the kids. The rides were out of this world, there was a ride called the *Tower of Power*. If you like adrenaline you cannot miss it! In this water slide of a height of 28m you can reach a speed of up to 80km/h, finishing the ride passing through a huge aquarium full of sharks and rays.

The three older girls were desperate to have a shot, and the first one down was Becks, she has no fear and always up for a challenge, but now the pressure was on Dad to follow suit. When you are walking up to the Tower of Power, that is when you realise how big the slide is, and the closer we got to the top, there were people walking down who had changed their minds and had to do the walk of shame by walking back down. Thankfully I was brave enough to go down the slide, what a speed, and my shorts/trunks were nearly ripped off at the end!

There were many highlights for me, but what I loved the most was seeing Joanne bursting with joy every day, with her having invested into our five awesome children, this was a reward to her for being a wonderful mother to them, yes I am indeed a blessed man.

The day that was difficult for me, was the one where Hannah had her first period at Siam Park, and it was me that was with her. I didn't have a clue what to do, poor Hannah ran off with a towel around her looking for her mum, boy I felt useless at that moment. Thank goodness Hannah found her mum quickly that day, and all was well going forward. If I could advise any new dads with girls, be more interested and get more knowledge about girls, especially once they become teenagers. Don't just leave it all to mum. The Tenerife adventure was an amazing experience, and all the family have wonderful memories.

Back home in Alford, one Sunday, Joanne had mentioned about getting a Chinese take-away for supper, it was a gorgeous evening, so I walked down to the Chinese. Walking around Alford, you are never bored by the beauty of the village, lovely scenery and many magnificent houses, most with stunning gardens, yes Alford is the place to be. As I approached the Chinese, which is situated on the Alford main street, a 'For Sale' sign caught my eye. I looked to my right and saw the most amazing house, I thought to myself, "Why have you not noticed this before", the front door was blue and

WILL YOUR ANCHOR HOLD

there was a fascinating door knocker, it was in the shape of a lion.

You see, a few weeks before, I had shared a message at a meeting about the Lion of Judah, which represents Jesus Christ. His name is Jesus, but He is also known as, "The Lion of Judah." This name originates back to the book of Genesis. The patriarch, Jacob ("Israel") gave this symbol to his tribe upon blessing his son Judah in Genesis 49:9. Jesus is a descendant of King David, who was from the Tribe of Judah. Seeing the Lion door-knocker, I heard what felt like an audible voice, it said "This is your house". This Holy Spirit moment was real and impacted into my very being. My first thoughts were, we cannot afford it, not a chance. My second thought was, there is no way that Joanne will leave the house in Burnbank.

Just a few weeks before I had shared at a meeting, and my talk was about the Lion of Judah, now I was looking a Lion door-knocker through spiritual eyes, the Holy Spirit prompting me to put in an offer of a house that we had never been in. I persuaded Joanne to come view the house, she wasn`t best pleased that I had asked to view the house, but the guy who owned the property was a lovely local man.

The house was much bigger inside than I thought, the downstairs was liveable, but there was a lot of work required for upstairs. The house had a massive living room, big kitchen, six bedrooms and another living room upstairs, and two bathrooms. This meant that with five kids, they would get a bedroom each, I had fallen in love with the house and could see us moving. Joanne on the other hand was not for it, she loved the house in Burnbank, and it was a more modern house, she had just settled into life at Burnbank.

Joanne said she would pray about the house on the Main Street, and a couple of days later she wanted another viewing, and this time she looked at through the eyes of faith. That next day we put in an offer, and this was rejected, which is usually the case with the first offer, to me it feels like a game between the solicitors, and they get the benefit more than the clients. We got the house on the third offer, and looking back it was a very fair price, we were over the moon and our moving date was 13th March 2013. The money from my dad's estate was used for the deposit for the house, I knew that it was something I had to do it for dad, it says in the Bible to honour your Father and Mother, which is the first commandment with a promise

My good friend and I moved all the household goods from Burnbank to the Main Street. There was snow on the ground that day, when we were lifting the large sofa to go upstairs, this was from the back steps, we lost grip on the sofa and it landed on the snow, a soft landing, with no damage thankfully, Joanne will only discover that while reading this!

WILL YOUR ANCHOR HOLD

Now all the kids had a room each, and they were all very excited in having their own space, yet while they were all growing up I can truly say that when they shared a room, they seemed closer as siblings. I remember having to share with my bothers growing up and we knew nothing different, good times too. We soon made the house a beautiful home, well mainly down to Joanne, she is the complete homemaker and has an exceptional gift in this department. She was loving seeing her vision coming together, bit by bit the rooms were painted to the thrill of the kids. Joanne`s dad is a qualified painter and decorator, a brilliant one at that, and he painted all the rooms.

Joanne and I are community orientated and we intended to be a positive influence in Alford by rolling up our sleeves and getting involved in any way we could. Joanne stated off with working in the Bistro, the perfect place for meeting people, and with Joanne`s outgoing personality, she soon got to know many folks from the village and surrounding areas. For me, it was the hard job in going to the pub, and coaching/playing football, again both excellent for getting to know the men of the village.

For church, we were still travelling to Aberdeen on a Sunday, which to me just didn't make sense, my heart was to do something in the village. Church had become boring, it felt like I was just going through the motions, and looking around the church building during a service, I was thinking, where are all the men? The working man, blue collar worker, basically someone like me, yes rough around the edges, but an open book. The mother in-law had noticed my disinterest at church, she has a gift in sensing the work of the Holy Spirit, and one day she handed me a book called *Why Men Hate going to Church*, written by David Murrow. This was a book that I devoured in a couple of days, and for those of you who really know me will know that it takes a long time for me to read a book. I will share more about this book in the next chapter.

Everything that was printed in this book described how I was feeling, from the worship in church to the length of the service. It was wearing me down, the wording of the songs felt like boyfriend music to me and that is not who I am, it was just too feely-touchy for me. The length of the service too was a battle, the time was 10:30 start to 12pm, yet many a time the service would finish at 12:30,or sometimes closer to 1pm. This totally turned me off, and it was then I did not ask, friends along to church, yes you got it, the service was too long. If I mentioned this to leadership then I was called negative, or my walk wasn't right with the Lord.

The above brings me back to leadership training that Joanne and I were involved in a couple of years earlier. There was a guest speaker all the way from America, well he was Australian but had planted a church in America, and the numbers went from 200 to 2,000 folks. The model he used was a church service for the unchurched, in a language they can understand, with worship songs that can connect with the man, and most importantly, the service will start on time and finish on time, with the service only an hour long. He shared that the mature Christian can access the Bible any day, can meet up with fellow believers through the week to study the Word, so Sunday should be an outreach, a place that you can bring a friend who will not feel like an alien. This guy was married with five kids (four boys and a gir)l, he was straight talking like many Aussies, but his heart for the Lord shone through him. This man would go around churches, video their service, then meet with the church leadership to equip them in going forward. Most church services are too long, especially for the men, and too many messages are not relevant and boring for the ordinary guy in the pew, they have to be challenged into the Kingdom of God.

Of all the leaders that shared on the Leadership training, he had the most impact on me, with the most vital component being that he didn't just talk it, he walked it… church on a Sunday has to be mainly for the lost, mature Christians have to be able to feed themselves. The pull of the Lord to do something different in the village of Alford was now burning in the hearts of both Joanne and I, we knew that his plans would unfold if we were both obedient to the call on our lives.

WILL YOUR ANCHOR HOLD

In Luke 11 v 28 - *He replied, "Blessed rather are those who hear the word of God and obey it."*

Living out a life of faith has to be about obedience, Joanne and I love the Lord, and we were getting ready to make the jump, but it had to be His timing. I am very impatient, and have made many mistakes with taking matters into my own hands. Now with Joanne aware of my personality, she had the wisdom and insight to keep me grounded, thank you Lord for a good wife, you gave me the best. With Joanne working in the pool and me as a Supervisor/Trainer in the Oil Industry, life was looking good. For the first since we were married we were now both making a good wage, with a wonderful work life balance, yes now we could build a future, with having the security in good jobs.

In Proverbs 16 v 9 - *In their hearts humans plan their course, but the LORD establishes their steps* (NIV)

The verse above is one that I have gone to many times in my Christian walk, and what was about to happen next was a humbling experience for me, yet threw me into a destiny in which I could only rely on God.

At work there were redundancies happening due to the downturn in the Oil Industry, every day there were people losing their jobs, and no one was safe. Deep in my spirit, God was preparing my heart for what was to come. May 15th, 2015 was the day that

WILL YOUR ANCHOR HOLD

my time with MI Swaco/Schlumberger came to an end. That morning there were HR and management all over the workplace, and one by one people were losing their jobs, with a few in tears, and no wonder.

Around 14:30 my line manager came into my office and said I had to go up to the boardroom, I quickly called Joanne to pray for me, but deep down I knew that my time was up. The way I handle a tense life situation is often through humour, I suppose it's an in-built defence mechanism to me. Walked into the boardroom, were the HR manager and MI Swaco Manager, both looking very tense. With my heart racing, I said "Well I guess I am not here for a pay rise", both the managers were fighting not to smile. In fact the HR manager said that she had seen me in a Street Pastor clip on Youtube, much needed sidetrack chat, but then business happened. I was told that I had a month left to work, and that a redundancy offer was on its way. After the chat I was told that I could leave straight away on full pay to look for another job. I thought I was doing okay, but taking off my boiler suit for the last time, one of my close friends came in to say goodbye, we both were emotional.

The harder bit was when I arrived home, Joanne and I gathered the kids. I told them the news in the best way I could have, but let's be honest, redundancy is brutal. Joanne and the girls got extremely emotional; the tears started to flow. Samuel, who

WILL YOUR ANCHOR HOLD

would have been seven years old, was saying from a child's perspective "it's okay, its okay."

Redundancy only really sinks in the days, weeks or even months after. I was feeling numb, disappointed, angry and more importantly a failure to my family. My faith was strong, but emotionally I was feeling weak, I'm thankful for my beautiful family though, they were fantastic throughout this difficult period. Work for any man is often where his identity is found, so like anyone, to lose this job was so disappointing.

It is strange, but I knew my number was up, that had been lack of communication from those at the top, so even though it was an individual shock to me, looking back there were obvious signs. After the initial shock I actually enjoyed the time off, which lasted for about three weeks. Then I knew that I would have to look for a job, since the redundancy money doesn't last long, especially with a big family to look after.

In that time of reflection, we got a new family member, her name was *Nala*, a beautiful working cocker spaniel. She was a stunning pup, and we had got her home when the girls were away for the weekend. The delight on their faces when meeting Nala is a favourite memory, she completed the Bain family. However it was time for me to look for work.

WILL YOUR ANCHOR HOLD

The way I was feeling I did not want to go back to the oil industry, the way the people were treated was shocking. While working in the company the HR people pushed for a duty of care which I totally agree with, yet after we were paid off it was like we were never there. In the meantime, I spoke with a friend who worked with the local roofing company and he was able to persuade his boss to take me on. Now going from the oil industry to the construction industry was a shock to the system. The oil industry was so health and safety conscious that you could not move without a strict risk assessment. Whereas the building trade was a different kettle of fish, basically get on with the job. The roofing guys were on a bonus, the quicker the job was complete the bigger the bonus. My initial thoughts were that this job would give me some breathing space to look for a long-term career change.

With being a labourer at the age of 46-year-old, it was certainly a huge shock to the system. Going from supervisor to labourer was a tough ask, not so much physically, but more emotionally and it tested my faith. Working for the roofing company was way out my comfort zone, with not knowing who I was going to work with and where the destination was going to be. The wage was obviously not as much as I earned in my previous job, but have to say that the owner was a good man and gave me a favourable wage, which was paid weekly.

WILL YOUR ANCHOR HOLD

The roofing company guys were all very hard workers and knew how to graft.

Joanne was amazingly patient with me during these hard times, she knew that I was struggling with the position. I remember while working at Aberdeen Royal Infirmary, there was a big team of roofers stripping the old felt roof. As the labourer my role was to wheelbarrow the mountain of old felt from the roof. I struggled to keep up with all the roofing team from the roof, it was really hard to wheelbarrow the felt into a skip. With The skip nearly full, I was asked to jump into the skip and crush the old felt to make room for more. That day while in the skip the tears started to flow and I shouted out to God saying "is this it?!" I felt sad and my mental health really suffered. With being in my late forties, I knew that getting a role like my previous one was nearly impossible, and anyway, the oil game was not my choice to go back too.

Many of my close friends had said that I should go into Ministry, both Christian and non-Christian knew my passion for people, living out my faith. God was working in the background, and soon the call on my life to follow His steps and not mine were about to unfold.

WILL YOUR ANCHOR HOLD

CHAPTER 15 - THE CALL

I am so thankful for the beautiful family that kept me going during these difficult years.

As I shared in the previous chapter, I thought that my days as a roofing labourer would last only a couple of months. Nowhere I was nearly two years later, still working as a labourer. In the interview before I started with the roofing company, the boss did say that I would learn on the job and would pick up the roofing skills. The reality was that the guys were always in a hurry to get the jobs done, and there was no time, or even a thought from the team, to train someone. This did my head in and even though in the early days I mentioned it to them, it fell on deaf ears. Eventually I just got on with the labouring duties, knowing that I had to look for something else that would get the creative juices flowing again. I'm not criticising these guys, they had worked in this environment all their lives, but the culture was wrong, there was no time for training unless you were going to work there for life, which nowadays is very unlikely. They even put up an advert in the school for a trainee roofer, and not one young person came forward, changed days indeed.

It was all coming to a head at home and at work, leaving early morning and not getting home till after six was wearing me and the family down. I was part of a roofing team to work up at St Fergus gas

WILL YOUR ANCHOR HOLD

terminal near Peterhead, which was a 62-mile round trip every day. It would be one hour twenty mins there and back, so not far off three hours travel time, making this an extremely long day.

My mood at home was not good, and the family tiptoed around me, which looking back was unfair. I would say that I was heading for depression, without hope. I had applied for many jobs without success, it's not easy getting a job in your late forties, and its usually who you know as well.

At St Fergus we were up on a massive flat roof, probably the size of a football pitch, it was huge. The health and safety regulations were over the top; yes we were up high, but the roof was flat and there was a four foot wall around us, no chance of anyone falling over. We also had to wear a harness, which had to be clipped onto a safety line, it was ridiculous really. My job was basically tidying up after the three other guys, and also cutting some roof insulation.

One day, up on the roof….. this actually sounds like a song lol….. there was a huge pile of roof insulation, I walked over to collect a board, but my safety line was not long enough. It was then that I sensed the Holy Spirit say "the Lord will cut you loose into your destiny", it was like an audible voice speaking to me, I felt my inner man get excited.

A couple of weeks after that encounter, Joanne said that there was a prophetic team coming from

WILL YOUR ANCHOR HOLD

America, they were from Bethel ministries. I didn't give Joanne much feedback, again not in a good headspace. The day arrived for this event, which was being held at Oasis church in the bridge of Don. Joanne asked if I was interested in going along, my reply was, "just go yourself, I am not interested". However as the day went on, I could feel the Holy Spirit nudging me, and just before Joanne was leaving to head to the Oasis Church, I said that I would be coming. Joanne being so gracious, she didn't say a word, she knew her husband and the inner battle I was going through.

We arrived at the Oasis Church, the car park was nearly full, there was a big crowd, in fact the church was full, with some folks having to stand at the back. The worship was inspiring and then the Pastor gave a powerful word, which created an atmosphere of faith, a place where the Holy Spirit could work. Then, the team from Bethel America stood up at the front of the church. There were five in total, four ladies and one man, which to me was a statement, the church in the UK is now roughly four to one in favour of the women.

What happened on this night had a huge impact in stepping out in faith….

Joanne, the mother in law and I were sitting together, about four rows from the front. The team from Bethel started to pick people out, the first two from the Bethel team prophesised over two from the

WILL YOUR ANCHOR HOLD

audience. The third Bethel member picked out Joanne, and gave her a powerful word, then the fourth Bethel member selected the Mother in law who was right beside Joanne, again with a powerful prophetic word.

Finally, it was now the fifth Bethel team member, she shared that she was not going to select from the audience, but that before she left America, she had asked the Lord for a name. When she shared the name, *Richard*, my heart was racing as I looked around and saw no one standing. As many of you know me as Ricky, my Christian name is Richard, so when I put my hand up, the whole place was in uproar, with three from the same family and same row now getting a prophetic word. Now, the word that this lady shared over me was a game changer, she first of all said that I was like Richard the lionheart, the Lion of Judah was roaring over me. The enemy had been on a mission to silence me, now was the season to roar, with the Lion of Judah roaring behind me, to be a lionheart for the Kingdom of God.

Well the Holy Spirit was evident, and I felt a supercharge in my Spirit, a powerful encounter with the Lord. Over the next few days Joanne, her Mum and I were all digesting our prophetic words, I listened to mine over and over, praying for direction. That same week, I received an email from the guy who headed up CVM Scotland saying he was leaving to become an Assistant Pastor. I quickly asked CVM if there was still a position in Scotland, and they said only part time.

At that time too God was trying to get my attention, I can be very stubborn, often not listening, doing it my way. On this particular Sunday I was involved in a car crash, it was totally my fault too, I went right into the back of a car that had stopped to turn right, it was indicating as well. Thankfully no one was hurt, and the couple in the car were okay, my car was smashed at the front, and I was unconscious for a few minutes. Honestly, I cannot remember the lead up to the crash, it was blank to me. I remember a good friend saying that it was time to listen to God and walk into your destiny.

Joanne and I prayed for wisdom as we sought the Lord on my next step. In my heart I had already made the move that I would be going full time in Kingdom work. I reached out to a few close Christian friends, and they had my back as I was getting ready to step out in faith. In the next few weeks I started an account with Stewardship, who are a Christian charity that help create accounts for Christian workers, who are then funded by individual supporters. Once I had received some funding, then I knew I was ready to quit my job with the roofing company.

The day arrived to hand in my notice, I was sitting in front of my Boss, and told him I was leaving his company to go and work for God. Well the look on

WILL YOUR ANCHOR HOLD

his face said it all, and like most folks, he just did not get it. He was a good man, and easy to get on with, and was totally respectful of my decision, although finding it hard to understand.

The last month with the roofing company seemed to go very slowly, and the guys I worked with just did not understand how I could leave a good paying job to work for a God most of them didn't believe in. My days working in the roofing company were not wasted, I made some good friendships, which are still going on to this day. I remember working with an older guy, and he asked me one Monday morning what I did at the weekend. I told him that I coached kids' football and watched *Match of the Day* on the Saturday evening, this was a tick box for him. When I said that I went to church he took a double take, saying that I did not look like a church goer. I did ask him what a church-goer looked like to him, he replied that they were usually older and female lol. We got onto the conversation of golf, the US Open had been played that weekend. I asked him if he noticed a sign with John 3 v 16 on it, he said that he had seen that.

Now this man was in his mid-60s, and when I said it was probably one of the most famous bible quotes, he still didn't have a clue. John 3 v 16 - *For God so loved the world that he gave his one and only Son, that whoever believes in him shall not perish but have eternal life.*

WILL YOUR ANCHOR HOLD

He was not interested in faith, but respected my lifestyle.

There was another time driving back to Alford, I was sitting in the middle of the roofing van with a guy either side me, when one of the guys received a phone call to tell him to hurry home. When this guy arrived home, he was given terrible news to say that his brother had committed suicide. That night I sent him a message just to say that I was a phone call away and that I would be praying for him and his family. In these horrible situations there are no words, just being a friend is the most valuable thing anyone can do.

I had many God chats with the team of roofers, most full of respect, but no interest in God. On my final day I bought lots of goodies and a thank you card to give to the lads. Most companies buy the person leaving a gift, but I knew in this company and its culture there would be no chance of that. The next day, I was asking myself, "are you mad?" yet I had this wonderful peace within me. I did what I loved to do, I danced in the kitchen with Nala our dog, truly excited about what lay ahead, desperate to start my role with Christian Vision for Men (CVM), there was a nation of men to reach for Christ.

In my first week with CVM and stepping out in faith I was hanging up curtains in the sitting room, when I heard something landing in the lobby at the front door. By the time I had laid down the curtains and went to open the front door, there was no one at the door. On the mat in the lobby was a large brown envelope, and unbelievably inside the envelope was a lot of cash, mainly £20 notes. Joanne and I counted out the money, and it came to £1,000. The timing of the money was again what Joanne and I have called many times, God`s timing, His timing is perfection. Thank you Jesus, what a boost to receive such a large gift. My heart was bursting with excitement, I was ready to take on this wonderful role with CVM.

What a start lay ahead, the director with CVM CYMRU doing what is called the three peak challenge to raise funds for the Charity. The three peak challenge is climbing the highest mountains in Scotland, England, Wales, which are Ben Nevis, Scafell Pike and Snowdon. The CVM CYMRU Director would also be carrying a wooden cross up and down these high mountains, a really brave commitment, and out of the box thinking.

He asked me to climb Ben Nevis with him to gently break me into the Scottish role, I was delighted to be asked and the thought of Climbing Ben Nevis with him was a wonderful way in starting off the CVM journey, a spiritual symbol too.

We met at a Hotel in Fort William, he came up with his friend who would help him with the three climbs, but he was not doing Ben Nevis, there was another friend that tagged along with us, he was

WILL YOUR ANCHOR HOLD

ready for Ben Nevis challenge. On the day, the weather was favourable and thankfully not too hot. On the journey up, we got a good response from the many folks on Ben Nevis, who were most intrigued seeing a guy carrying a cross up Ben Nevis. We had plenty of rest breaks, and I offered to carry the cross, but CVM CYMRU man was not having it, this was his journey to raise as much as possible for CVM. At the top, the view was amazing, a clear blue sky and we could see way into the horizon. This was a hard climb, especially for the man from Wales, he did unbelievable to carry the cross all the way up, what a phenomenal effort, he has such a strong work ethic, a man of great perseverance. We all held the cross and prayed over Scotland, and got our photo taken at the summit too, an experience I will never forget. On the way down again we had wonderful conversations, and some folks ignored us too, but this didn't affect us too much, as you know the cross can be offensive to the many who don't believe in Jesus. The highlight on the way down was encountering a group of four skinheads with tattoos. When we first saw these muscle-bound guys coming towards us, our first thoughts were, here we go, some mickey taking is about to take place. Well, of all the folks we encountered that day, these guys were full of praise and admiration. They even offered us money for the cause, they loved the fact seeing Christian men rising up and being a great witness for our faith in Jesus Christ. Many men want to see faith in action, and for them seeing a man carry a cross up and down Ben Nevis, with two Christian brothers beside him, was an awesome sight for them. I still smile to myself when I look back and remember these lovely guys, who looked hard, yet their hearts were soft, and they had a positive impact on the three of us. This encounter gave us a huge lift, especially Mr Wales, he now had an extra spring in his step, and we were praying and thanking the Lord for the final descent on Ben Nevis. The CVM CYMRU gent went on to complete England and finally Snowdon in his homeland, what an effort and brilliant achievement, he raised a few thousand for CVM, well done that man.

I embraced the Ben Nevis experience, since I'm always up for a physical challenge too. I did what is called the Wolf Trek in 2014, walking 43 miles from Forres all the way to the Cairngorm Mountain, now what a walk this was, walking all through the night, and you know what….it rained all the time! The blisters were agony.

In 2015 I did the Tough Mudder with a friend, which was another exciting adventure, and well named in the tough and mud…

A few weeks after the Ben Nevis climb, I had my first experience of the CVM Gathering in a field in Swindon, 'what is *The Gathering'* you may ask?

The CVM Gathering, as described by the President of the movement, is a combination of *Songs of*

WILL YOUR ANCHOR HOLD

Praise and *Top Gear*; a weekend of camping, fun, banter, worship, bible teaching, football, axe throwing, zip wire, amazing cars, big tent atmosphere, beers, in fact everything a man would enjoy. Obviously, the main purpose of the weekend is bringing men to Christ.

CVM have a winning formula, connecting with men in a way that's basically user friendly, going into their world with an understandable message, going after the working-class guy who has no interest in church, yet they are intrigued by Jesus Christ.

That first weekend experience for me was amazing, I loved it all, the stunning weather helped too, because the previous year was a wash out.

On the Saturday evening, there was a call to the men in the huge tent to come forward and bow their knee at the rustic wooden cross that was positioned at the front of the main stage. There were over one hundred guys who came forward, some with a first-time commitment, and many more to get the fire back in their Christian walk with Jesus. After these guys had come forward, they were guided to the prayer tent, a time for them to have a one to one chat, and hopefully a follow up plan, so they could be planted into a local church group or in a place of fellowship with like-minded men. Often the easy bit is to put your hand up or step forward and say the prayer, yet most men often slip away after an event, so it's vital they are discipled and placed in an environment to grow in their Faith.

As many of you will know from experience, after any large-scale event, where the adrenalin has been pumping, and the weekend was full on, you are back home before you know it, and you feel a bit flat. This is how I felt a couple of days after coming home, with my CVM journey of to a whirlwind start with the Ben Nevis climb and first CVM Gathering, now I was back home asking the question "What is next?"

Now I had to look at the spreadsheet that had been passed onto me with all the CVM groups connected in Scotland, there were officially twelve. Now I had all the details on the spreadsheet to get in touch with the group leaders, sad to say that out of the twelve groups, there were only now three active CVM groups in the whole of Scotland. For the other nine groups, some leaders had moved on and the group was no more, others had decided not to be part of CVM, even the church who the previous CVM Scotland man attended didn't want to carry on under the CVM banner. My heart actually began to sink, 'what is happening here?' I thought, only three active groups in the whole of Scotland, have I made a huge mistake? am I losing it?!

As a father of five children, was I in danger of putting my whole family at risk to chase a dream? Am I selfish? these were the thoughts running through my head, and I knew many folks who were thinking along these lines too. Thankfully Joanne as usual was right beside me, cheering me on, she reassured me that there was a call on my life, to do something that most will never fully understand. Even while writing this, I want to say a huge, huge thank you to my wonderful wife and beautiful children. It was not just me who took this massive step of faith, my family have come with me, they have been fantastic in helping me journey in a world that just doesn't understand or maybe even appreciate a life of faith.

North of Scotland Director CVM was my official title, the role was to engage with churches in the land, to either help start a church mens group or if the church had one, hopefully to partner the group to CVM, creating a movement of men in Scotland. It sounds easy, but the reality was totally different, I was about to realise how hard this role with CVM was going to be. First of all, I emailed all the churches in Aberdeen, reaching out, praying for favourable replies. Unfortunately the response was not good, in fact I would use the word terrible, one church leader came back saying that they were under the CVM banner, but now they wanted out. Another said they were happy with their in-house men's group, but had no interest in being part of a bigger movement, and I didn't hear back from most of the churches. On the plus side, I did manage to start three groups in Aberdeen, out of the three groups, one was the church I was attending and the other was a really good friend`s church. Yes they must have felt sorry for me, this is honestly how I felt. My character is one of perseverance, and I was ready for the challenge, believing that God would open doors with churches throughout Scotland, 'bring it on!' was what I was shouting to myself.

In the summer of 2017, CVM Scotland went along to the *Refuel* Festival in Fochabers, a beautiful estate in the North of Scotland was the location, and this was my first outing at a Christian Festival with CVM. In the Market tent, each ministry represented was given a table and chair in the Tent, this was where we could promote our ministries, CVM have a lot of wonderful resources, all to do with reaching men. The atmosphere at *Refuel* is brilliant, many wonderful people coming from not just Scotland, but from all over the UK. They come for the week, and as the title of the Festival says, to be fuelled back up, a time to refresh and enjoy the amazing worship and teaching from the speakers that were there for the week.

The only downside was that CVM are an outreach movement, with an evangelistic vision to help equip churches to reach men. What I saw at Refuel was a huge ratio in favour of the ladies. As well as this the age range was older and very much middle-class folks, and they all embraced the week and had an awesome time in the beautiful surroundings.

WILL YOUR ANCHOR HOLD

For me in the Market place tent, most folks gave a smile and walked past the CVM table, one or two stopped for a chat, and the majority agreed that there is a void of men, especially the young working class male within the church in Scotland. That week, I sold between 10-15 books, not great for a week, but small steps, and it is all about the ones and two`s. I went along to a few of the teaching sessions, and was blessed with the teachers of the word, and this what realistically Refuel is about, filling up the Christians and blessing their walks with the Lord. The team who run Refuel are all dedicated amazing folks with a huge heart for the Kingdom, the vision to see people changed for Jesus.

For the remainder of 2017 with CVM Scotland, we had a roadshow in Aberdeen, with over 120 guys turning up, a really blessed day in the city of Aberdeen. Nearly all Christian men though, which is good, but the CVM vision is for the Christian Men to reach out to non-churched friends. The huge problem with this, is that most christian men don't have unchurched mates, now that is the real issue in a nutshell.

On the home front, we were getting by each month on the financial front, thankful to be able to pay the bills and still enjoy the family at home. Joanne was working at the swimming pool, she did lifeguarding and was a swimming teacher as well. She is a born teacher, she loved the job, yet like many people, hated the politics at the pool, unfortunately where she worked had a horrible bullying culture, which even to this day has not changed.

Katie had joined the Police, I was so proud of her going straight from the school into the Police force, an amazing achievement, proud dad moment! Hannah was doing her Hairdressing apprenticeship, doing brilliant, but struggling with the bitchy atmosphere in the workplace, again proud dad! Rebecca was still at school, again doing well and proud dad! Rachel at school too, and she was excelling in the football, a gifted young player, proud dad! Samuel was still in the Primary school, a typical young loom, proud dad!

The above theme is 'proud dad', all my family make me proud, a blessed man indeed, and as someone once said to me, whatever you do in this world, your five kids will be your biggest achievement, correct!

Now 2018 with CVM was a good one, a couple of more groups starting up and a roadshow in Perth, around 100 guys going to that one, and I got the chance to share the message too, so I started a men`s group in Aberdeen, called Credo Men, set in the Credo café, John Street. The vision was to bring the men of faith in the city together for a once a month meeting, a safe place for the guys to get to know one another, through friendship, fun, food and a wee message at the end to encourage them. The first night there was twenty four men who turned up, and back then I thought this was disappointing, my hope was for at least thirty, we had invited many guys from the different churches throughout the city. Like I have shared already, most Christian men don't seem to have non-Christian friends, and the churches struggle to mingle with one another, our night was Wednesday, and the majority of reasons that the men could not make it, was due to the fact they had their own church night on a Wednesday. I was thinking to myself, surely you can give up one Wednesday in the month to do outreach. I was really thankful to have three or four guys who helped to lead these nights, two guys in particular, both of whom I still meet and pray with.

CVM were back at Refuel, this time in a much bigger tent, thanks to a good friend who helped with the finances to make this possible. This guy has been by my side ever since, a really great man who sees me for who I am, warts and all, now that is a friend who has your back. Our Tent was big one, thanks to my friend who helped with funding, we had the Credo men gear to, Dart board, Giant Jenga, Table tennis, weights and even a tug of war rope. Again, the week itself was a tough one trying to engage with an older audience, who were at *Refuel* to be blessed and have much needed rest, which I fully understand and appreciate.

The real wonderful blessing that week, apart from the most amazing weather, was the friendly guys we encountered from *Teen Challenge*, 'what is Teen challenge' you may ask? Teen Challenge UK is a registered charity and operates nationally to help young people who have developed life controlling problems, especially drug and alcohol addictions, and also to offer preventative help to those who may be in danger of doing so.

Teen Challenge UK started in 1968 and now works in fifteen locations in England, Wales, Northern Ireland and Scotland. Teen Challenge London and Teen Challenge Strathclyde grew out of Teen Challenge UK and are affiliated works. The goal of Teen Challenge UK is to help people become mentally sound, physically well, emotionally balanced, socially adjusted & spiritually alive.

These young guys actually made our week, seeing them now in good shape mentally, physically, emotionally and of course spiritually was inspirational. I have a huge admiration to those who run these life-changing charities, full respect. The lads hung around our tent all week, they felt comfortable with the games, weights and fun challenges, and yes, they were all working class, again the connection was mutual, a common theme together.

The vision in Scotland was to take the CVM Gathering that is in a field in Swindon to Scotland, that is still the hope and prayer. In 2018 the summer weather was truly remarkable, and working with CVM, a busy year for connecting, networking and

WILL YOUR ANCHOR HOLD

looking to build the movement in Scotland, what I did learn was to keep persevering. I went over to the Western Isles to to do a winning men presentation with the guys from the different churches on the Island, the place of revival (the Lewis revivals took place there in from 1949 to 1953)…

The minister at Barvas, James Murray MacKay (who sadly died in 1954), invited Duncan Campbell (his second choice) to come over and minister, but he was refused due to Campbell's busy schedule. Now there were two elderly sisters, one blind, who were amazing intercessors, who the minister respected greatly, and they told him that Campbell would come, so they and the church prayed and he arrived in Barvas, Lewis on December 7th 1949. There is a myth across the internet, that came from Campbell's writings, that the Smith sisters prayed in the revival and were solely responsible for Campbell's arrival. This story is untrue, the whole Island was praying in the revival and the whole church for Campbell to come.

As Christians today, we do seek and pray for revival again across the Nation of Scotland, we have to get back to be a nation of prayer, that is when we will see a real revival, now what a beautiful thought.

The call on my life now felt real, I was living out of faith, totally reliant on the Lord, and learning all the time, the good and the not so good.

WILL YOUR ANCHOR HOLD

On the family front, our youngest daughter's football team won the Scottish Cup, it was the under 13 age group. A team from Alford, Aberdeenshire called Donside had become Scottish Cup holders, what an amazing achievement, a very talented bunch of girls. Proud Dad moment, seeing my daughter lift the Scottish Cup!

In late 2018 I went down to Cliff College in the Peak District, England, to attend the Men's Ministry course run by CVM. This was a week's course, equipping the church for evangelism and mission. There were great speakers that week, men who had a heart, vision and life experience in sharing how to reach the nation of men, in church and those outside the building. I embraced the whole week, met new friends and learnt a lot of valuable stuff to help engage the men. To finish off this chapter, I have shared my project from that week. I had to answer a question, which was : name two issues that the church and help the men of this nation with? The two issues were gambling and pornography, and this includes the men inside the building too, I had to write a minimum of 3000 words, which to me, was a huge challenge. I was delighted to get my certificate, and my marks were a B+, for me that was a miracle. Hope you enjoy my essays on Gambling and the P-word….

INTRO

WILL YOUR ANCHOR HOLD

In society today, there are many addictions which affect men (and women).

As someone who works for a Christian Men's movement, my role is to investigate how we can engage with men in modern Britain, helping men to first of all talk about issues that they often keep to themselves.

The purpose of this assignment is to reflect on two key issues facing men in society, and how the Christian church can respond, support and offer ministry into those issues.

Addiction comes in many forms, for example, alcohol or drug addiction, which come under substance addictions.

Behavioural addictions can vary and include eating disorders, sex and co-dependency, shopping, gaming and gambling.

Addiction is the term given to a pattern of behaviour that causes negative consequences for the individual. Most people assume that addiction refers only to those who have compulsive need for a particular substance such as alcohol or drugs. However, it is possible to become addicted to almost anything. To be clear, this condition occurs when a person continues to do something despite knowing that it will have an adverse impact on his or her life. Due to the various causes and triggers, there are many different types of addictions.

WILL YOUR ANCHOR HOLD

The two issues I want to explore further are gambling and pornography, they are addictions that are destroying men in society today.

How can the church respond with support and offer ministry?

The church has to firstly recognize this is not just a secular problem, gambling and especially pornography are present in the `church building`, so these issues have to be dealt with in-house before the church is able to help those outside the Christian world.

The church has to be able to stand strong, and the Christians have to be transparent and vulnerable with one another, we need to be healed before we can help the men in the secular world.

In Ephesians ch5v 13 – But everything exposed by the light becomes visible and everything that is illuminated becomes a light.

Gambling and pornography are sinful addictions, and scripture says that sin does not like to be exposed.

People avoid God all the time. Sin keeps us entangled in bondage, while shame and guilt keep them right there in the heat of it.

So as a man who will be fifty next year, I have come across many men who have and are still affected by pornography and gambling. I have been affected by pornography and gambling, so I know from a personal experience how damaging these two major addictions can be to men in all walks of life.

I remember when we had a Men`s night at church and one of the Leaders shared about his pornography addiction, none of the men knew how to deal with what the Leader shared, and we all changed the subject. It was a cry for help from the church leader and we sadly ignored it.

The church men have to be accountable first and foremost, then trained to help the men who are crying out, and often feel no one is listening to them.

Gambling

Gambling is the wagering of money or something of value (referred to as the "stakes) on an event with an uncertain outcome, with the primary intent of winning money or material goods. Gambling thus requires three elements be present: consideration, risk(chance), and a prize. The outcome of the wager is often immediate, such as a single roll of dice, a spin of a roulette wheel, or a horse crossing the finish line, but longer time frames are also common, allowing wagers on the outcome of a future sports contest or even an entire sports season. (Gambling Wikipedia).

WILL YOUR ANCHOR HOLD

The gambling culture has been with men since the beginning of time, even Roman soldiers gambled who would get Jesus` clothes.

Matthew Ch. 27 v 35-37.

The soldiers nailed Jesus to a cross. Then the soldiers gambled with dice to decide who would get Jesus` clothes. The soldiers sat there and continued watching Jesus. The soldiers put a sign above Jesus head with the charge against him written on it. The sign said: This is JESUS, THE KING OF THE JEWS.

How sad and repulsive that the Roman soldiers would even gamble on the clothing of our saviour Jesus Christ.

Basically, men who are ardent gamblers will bet over anything, this shows how serious this addiction gets a hold on the men.

When I was 15/16 years old, I went to the local games room in my hometown of Stromness, Orkney. There was the juke box, pool tables, sweets and soft drinks, as well as the video games. In the corner of the games room, was the fruit machine, with Jack pot prize £10, this was a lot of money back in the mid 80`s, and I was addicted to this fruit machine, on it every chance I could get. In fact, I knew this machine too well, could even anticipate the sequences and would often win top prize when the 3-x sevens appeared.

WILL YOUR ANCHOR HOLD

My addiction got so bad that I would pinch money from my Mum's purse and it wasn't coppers I stole, £10, sometimes even £20's, still look back on these day's in shame for what I did.

Eventually my Mum and Dad confronted me on the missing money, so I admitted to my gambling problem, my parent's got the lad who owned the pool room to ban me from the games room. So thankfully I did not enter that facility again and have not been on a fruit machine since.

Parental boundaries are so important.

Sport, especially the footballing world has been awash with betting, in 1923 Littlewoods first offered pool betting outside Old Trafford.

After the betting and gaming act of 1960, betting shops were legalised from May the following year. In 2001 the betting tax was abolished. The Government's tax of bookmakers previously meant that the bookies passed on a 9% tax to punters. On 1st January 2001 the changes came into effect. The rules around football betting specifically are further relaxed, with the 'minimum trebles' rule dropped in 2002. Punters can now bet on single matches rather than the minimum of three as before.

I know it's not just football that men bet over, but I simply want to share what I have encountered on my own journey with the football world.

WILL YOUR ANCHOR HOLD

Having played football since as far as I can remember, I love the game…

I did not notice a gambling culture until I hit the Academy way back in 1981, this is when I saw the lads at school betting on games from the weekend, myself included.

My family were all football mad and my Dad was regular with the Littlewoods football coupon, but he was always a canny Aberdonian and certainly didn`t have a gambling addiction.

So, from the early 80`s right through to 2018, I have seen the damage gambling can do to those close to me and around me. From card schools, betting shops right through to online gambling, I`ve seen the damage this can do to a man with an addictive personality.

The Pastor (who is a great friend) of the church I attend, sent me his dad`s testimony about the gambling world. His dad used to own a bookies shop, a very successful business, it was only when his dad gave his life to the Lord that he felt under so much conviction from the Holy Spirit, he eventually sold the business.

Below are his own words.

"However, there is no doubt that gambling does give a `rush and can provide excitement. This soon wears off, but can be replicated by repetition. People do win and to many this gives them some status amongst others in the workplace. The workplace could be a place of social activity as well amongst regulars. In the long run through a regular gambler will always lose". Ref- Pastor's Dad (Barry Dennis).

The above is a true statement, in the long run, it is always the bookies who are the winners and yes the Government are winners too, from fiscal year 2000/01 to fiscal year 2017/18, betting and gaming tax receipts totalled almost £31.5 billion, an incredible windfall for HMRC.

It's the man on the street, the average working men whose lives are often ruined by the gambling addiction. Many men go onto lose jobs, houses, families and even many are lost to suicide. One in fivemen struggling with problem gambling are almost 25 x more likely to attempt suicide than the general population.

How can the church help the men in the UK with their gambling addiction?

Church Initiative has created a 13- week video series for churches entitled Chance to Change: Christ-Centred Gambling Recovery. This resource empowers churches to reach problem gamblers in their communities.

The men in the church who have a gambling problem need to share with the guys who are close

WILL YOUR ANCHOR HOLD

to them. This can be done on a one to one basis or, like we started in our own church, with life-groups.

The life-group I am part of is for men, the Pastor felt guided to have same gender life-groups. This gives the men the chance to be real and they will feel more comfortable to talk about issues in a trusting environment.

The church has to become a safe environment where guys with a gambling addiction will feel loved and supported, but also challenged to be real.

PORNOGRAPHY

My first experience of pornography was when my friend showed me his Dad`s stash of pornography magazines in the garden shed.

At the age of twelve years old, this was certainly an eye opener for me, well I think my eye`s nearly popped out of my eye sockets. From this young age I would have to say this was my journey into the world of pornography. That shed was a regular haunt for me, to have a vivid look at the graphic pictures and also read all the stories of sexual adventures that were beyond my own experience at that time.

So back in 1981 it was through glossy magazines that the young men would have their first fix of porn.

WILL YOUR ANCHOR HOLD

Pornography is nothing new, cave drawings showing exaggerated genitalia and fertility rituals have been found in various countries around the world dating from as early as 2000 BC. It seems that mankind has always been fascinated by sex and sexuality, and, using the crudest of implements, have attempted to portray it. Human sexuality has also played a profound role in the belief systems of most of the world's cultures throughout the ages and in all major religions. When you consider that the gift of our sexuality allows us to perform the ultimate miracle and create life, there's little wonder that we both revere it and fear it. (Ref p28 Confronting Porn by Paula Hall).

Our modern world is ruled by the internet and nearly everyone has access to a mobile phone, with this there is a huge epidemic issue with access to pornography. It is well documented that early growth of www in 1990's was due largely to online porn.

One in twenty fivewebsites are pornographic and about one in eight web searches are for erotic content.In 2016, a SINGLE porn website reported 23 billion visits a year.

It is clear that the Pornography problem is out of control and this addiction is destroying our lives and values.When I worked in the Oil industry as a Workshop Supervisor, the younger staff would

WILL YOUR ANCHOR HOLD

unashamedly show pornography to one another from their mobile phones.

This would happen in the workshop canteen and in the workshop itself, yet if I walked in, the guys would quickly shut their phones off.

Even though I was the Supervisor I felt that I had no backing from my line manager, who would say "It's harmless fun Ricky, the lads are not harming anyone", sadly I knew that was not true.

So, from what we see, many from the world, view, see Porn as just part of modern society and we just have to put up and accept this destructive addiction.

The Naked Truth website (www.nakedtruthproject.com) remind usof the page three era, which were pictures of beautiful ladies in the newspapers, topless ladies, I remember them well.

Today the men are searching for more than topless photos, 56% of men said that their taste in porn had become increasingly extreme or deviant often creating problems in real relationships, as fantasy never matches reality.

Pornography can and does ruin relationships and ultimately the intimacy of a marriage. With intimacy gone in a relationship, then many couples will eventually separate.

WILL YOUR ANCHOR HOLD

Here is some of a testimony from a lovely Christian lady we know, below is her own words about the destructive effect of porn :

"It soon got to the point where intimacy in our marriage was scarce. How could I compete with the images that were so heavily engrained in his mind and the expectation that that's what it should be like in real life. Then this was his disappointment. And the degrading thoughts that were running through my mind, of not being enough, beautiful, sexy, slim, daring enough, only created a vicious circle for both of us. The less I would respond to his "needs" the more he would turn to porn and vice versa"!

So how can the Church respond, support and offer ministry to deal with pornography?

Last year my Pastor asked if I would like to go to a conference in Glasgow called the *P Word*, my answer was what does the P stand for? He explained that this was about Pornography, that this was for all the churches across Scotland.

There was a huge turnout at the conference, church Pastors and leaders from all over Scotland. So it showed that the church recognised that there was a massive problem in society with Pornography.

Yes, I am writing about Porn addiction that men struggle with, but at the P Word conference the first testimony was from a young female worship leader, who had come through her porn addiction.

WILL YOUR ANCHOR HOLD

So, this sexual addiction has contaminated both genders and all age groups.

However, I want to focus on the men and this last section is on how the Christian church can help men with their pornography issue.

What I took away from the P word conference was some fantastic material, including a book named *Confronting Porn*, written by Paula Hall, who is a psychotherapist and author. Paula is widely recognised as the UK's leading expert in the field of sex and porn addiction and frequently speaks in the media as well as training other professionals.

Confronting Porn is a valuable tool in helping a man through his addiction, from facing the truth, to finding freedom in Christ- Read John ch8 v 31-32.

For men of faith we need to be open and honest with each other, and if we have a porn habit, then this has to be out in the open, so you will need accountability partners.

For myself, a friend offered to set up an online resource called www.covenanteyes.com.

Covenant eyes provide internet accountability and filtering software, this will show your search history, so it is vital to be accountable to someone you can trust. This tool is not to shame men but let him know he is not alone, and help is available. This leads to freedom rather than bondage.

WILL YOUR ANCHOR HOLD

Addiction thrives in secrecy and shame and the most effective way of counteracting that is to step out of the shadows and into the light.

CONCLUSION

The two key issues that men are facing in Society are pornography and gambling.

As a Christian man who works for Christian Vision for Men, we are always looking for ways we can help men navigate through life.

In the introduction for this essay, I covered that addiction comes in many forms, alcohol, drugs, also behavioural addictions like eating disorders, sex, shopping, gaming and gambling.

Pornography and gambling were the addictions that I experienced for myself, so much of the essay is from a personal journey.

The heart of the Christian church is to disciple, grow and multiply their congregations, that the body of Christ can be trained, equipped to help a lost world.

The church help communities, with having a strong foundation with prayer warriors who will pray for their church and the ministries that the church have within the building.

WILL YOUR ANCHOR HOLD

So, the first thing that must happen is for the church leaders to recognise we have to warfare in prayer against pornography and gambling.

Like I shared in the Pornography issue, no one seems to want to chat about this addiction, the gambling one would be easier to talk about.

Hebrews Ch 4 v 15-16

For we do not have a high priest who is unable to empathize with our weakness, but we have one who has been tempted in every way, just as we are, yet he did not sin. Let us then approach God`s throne of grace with confidence, so that we may receive mercy and find grace to help us in our time of need.

We all have a weakness in life, no matter who you are, well all fall short, men need to know that there is mercy and grace from the Christian church, and people who will empathize with them so that we in the body of Christ, will journey all the way with the men who are crying out for help from the addictions of Pornography and Gambling.

With working for Christian Vision for Men, I have helped start a men`s night once a month in a café in Aberdeen. We get between 20 to 30 guys from all walks of life coming along, from professional, blue collar workers, right through to those who are struggling to find work. There are a few of the men who you can see struggle with alcohol, drugs and depression, these three you can detect and know the issue.

Pornography and Gambling are hidden, there is no way of knowing who has an issue unless they share about it.

So, going forward, we know there is specialized help there. Going to the P word conference in Glasgow was an eye-opener, but I believe that God goes before and because I went to the conference, I received valuable materials that can help me, church and Christian Vision for Men to help the men from Porn addiction.

Gambling, there is help there, from books, online help, like GamCare Uk`s national organisation for gambling problem help.

There is Christian help for gambling, like Christians against gambling, there goal is recovery from addiction to Christ.

Mark Ch8 v36 :

For what shall it profit a man if he shall gain the whole world, and lose his soul?

WILL YOUR ANCHOR HOLD

CHAPTER 16 - STILL IN THE GAME

I am laughing to myself now, since I called this chapter 'still in the game', maybe more like *Still Game* the comedy series, and one of my favourite TV shows. It's hilarious, my go to show when I need some laughter medicine.

Now into 2019 and another productive year with CVM, as well as in my own journey of faith. We never stop learning and in April of that year I had an incredible, yet daunting, experience doing the XCC, which stands for 'Xtreme Character Challenge'. The main reason for doing the XCC was to raise funds for CVM, as a charity we were encouraged as a team to raise funds for the movement. XCC is run by a Christian movement called the 4th Musketeer, which inspires men to serve their King through Extreme Character Challenges (XCCs) and fight injustice through charity runs, cycling and hiking. This was how XCC 2019 was advertised – "Join us in the Scottish Highlands in April 2019 for an XCC - a mind body soul adventure - an active and challenging endurance event for men, out in the wild, that changes lives."

XCC 1.0 - "Search and Discover". This XCC is designed for men looking for answers to big questions. Through a Mind Body Soul Adventure, you will challenge and explore what it means to live as a man in the modern world. Bring your brain, your issues, your life, your boots, your struggles, your successes; bring yourself.

WILL YOUR ANCHOR HOLD

XCC 2.0 "Decision Time". A Mind, Body Soul Adventure for men connected to church who want to go deeper in faith and value inspiration. Are you looking for a challenge? Are you ready to live for purpose? It's time to change. It's time to become the man you were made to be.
Both XCC's will start on Thursday 11th April 2019 (17h00 at Edinburgh Airport or on location at 20h00). Both events will finish by 12h00 on location on Sunday 14th April. Coaches will depart immediately and therefore those flying from Edinburgh Airport will be dropped off no later than 15h00.

There were a few of us from Aberdeen and the shire who drove up to Loch Tay to meet many others who were looking to push ourselves to the limit, but not knowing what was in front of us. The guy who led the 4M movement gave us instructions and rules before we set off on the hike. We had to hand over all electronic gadgets, including my Fitbit. I was hoping to break daily records with all the walking that lay ahead. He also said no snacks, because we were given rations for the days ahead, and that anyone who had snacks in their rucksacks were encouraged to hand them in. I had packed away a large bag of mars bars for snacking, and my first thought was, nobody will know, we need snacks. Aye, but the conviction from the Holy Spirit was burning in me, so I handed in all my mars bars, with a tear in my eyes I will say, I was gutted.

WILL YOUR ANCHOR HOLD

There were well over one hundred men, and we were in groups of ten, a good number to walk with, we all knew this was going to be a tough few days. Four days and three nights in the Perthshire hills, and the weather was dry, but not very warm. We all set off at a fast pace, but as we started to walk up the first hill, the speed started to drop and the happy chitter, chatter had disappeared, it was sinking in that there was no turning back, the hard work had only just begun. Over the following days and nights, we were all pushed to our limits, emotionally, physically, spiritually too. We walked for miles, encouraging one another onwards, leaving no one behind. The way 4M has created this amazing experience, you have to say they left no stone unturned, they thought of everything. There were inspirational, honest talks, on subjects like the Father`s heart, and on addictions, being ashamed of Jesus, and much more.

The talk about addictions was what got a lot of our group chatting, the addiction talk was on the Saturday, so we had been together a couple of days, getting confident in each other's company. The guy who I was walking with at the time, shared to with me about his online gambling addiction, something he was ashamed about. Having the courage to share and being vulnerable are the first steps in getting help. I was there to listen without judgement, I was simply there alongside him, to help him overcome the issue.

WILL YOUR ANCHOR HOLD

Every talk that was shared by an individual was spot on, impacting at least one member from our group of ten. I was really impressed with the creative journey that the 4M guys had planned for this epic adventure. There were lots of activities over the days, and the one that stood out for me was the one when we had to share the load of our partner. We had to take off our rucksack and give it to our partner, who would carry his own rucksack, as well as mine, then we would swap over. For men we are not good at asking for help, having a friend carry our burdens for a while, taking the load from us to heal. I'm not going to share too much more about the experience, because we were signed to secrecy, and the 4M movement would love more men to give it ago.

What I will share is doing church on the hillside on Loch Tay… now this moment will never leave me. I could have shared the word 'church service', but this was a gathering of men, who had shared life together, over four days, three nights, being vulnerable, pushed to their limits and now standing on a hillside about to worship the Lord. That morning, the weather was good, the sun was rising over the mountain across Loch Tay. We could feel the warmth of the sun on our faces, as we were about to do church in a way that seemed so natural and authentic. The worship was truly amazing, and the song that got to every man was *Good, Good Father* by Chris Tomlin. Now this broke all the men on the hillside that morning, not a dry eye, and the

WILL YOUR ANCHOR HOLD

men were fully engaged in worship. Here are the lyrics for Good, Good Father-

Oh, I've heard a thousand stories
Of what they think You're like
But I've heard the tender whisper
Of love in the dead of night
And You tell me that You're pleased
And that I'm never alone

You're a good good Father
It's who You are, it's who You are, it's who You are
And I'm loved by You
It's who I am, it's who I am, it's who I am

Oh, and I've seen many searching
For answers far and wide
But I know we're all searching
For answers only You provide
'Cause You know just what we need
Before we say a word

You're a good good Father
It's who You are, it's who You are, it's who You are
And I'm loved by You
It's who I am, it's who I am, it's who I am

WILL YOUR ANCHOR HOLD

'Cause You are perfect in all of Your ways
You are perfect in all of Your ways
You are perfect in all of Your ways to us

Oh, it's love so undeniable
I, I can hardly speak
Peace so unexplainable
I, I can hardly think
As You call me deeper still
As You call me deeper still
As You call me deeper still
Into love, love, love

You're a good good Father
It's who You are, it's who You are, it's who You are
And I'm loved by You
It's who I am, it's who I am, it's who I am

You are perfect in all of Your ways
You are perfect in all of Your ways
You are perfect in all of Your ways

Now what a song to break the hearts of the men, and He is the perfect Father, and we are so loved by Him. After the worship finished, one of the leaders asked a couple of questions, the first one being "who is a Christian?" 90% of the hands went up. Then he asked, "Please be honest here, how many of you willingly go to church on a Sunday?", out of nearly one hundred and fifty guys there were only

WILL YOUR ANCHOR HOLD

five hands that went up. Wow, now this did not shock me in the slightest, with being all over Scotland banging the CVM drum without much success, the numbers are about right I would say.

Now let's go back to that book I was talking about in the previous chapter, called *Why Men Hate Going to Church*, a book written by David Murrow, who is an award- winning television producer and writer based in Alaska. He is director of 'Church for Men', an organization that helps congregations reconnect with the world's largest unreached people group. The first edition of *Why Men Hate Going to Church* was an instant Christian bestseller, with more than 100,000 copies in print. His efforts have spawned articles in the New York Times, the Wall Street Journal, and the Chicago Tribune, to name a few. He has featured on PBS, the NBC Nightly News, and the Fox News Channel, talking about the gender gap. What I have seen and learned on my own journey is that there definitely is a gender gap, in this book there are case studies and examples about ordinary men who see no reason for going to a church building.

No 1 Man – "I can worship God better out in nature than I can sitting in a church building".

There is an amazing picture of a guy in a fishing boat, the quote said "religion is a guy in church thinking about fishing. Relationship is a guy out fishing thinking about God." (Amen!). I remember my daughter Rebecca asking why her Bampa didn't

WILL YOUR ANCHOR HOLD

go to church, he answered by saying that he believed in God, but would rather meet him on a mountain. Rebecca replied "Well the next time you hike up a mountain, I pray that you meet God there"

No 2 Man – "I just don't feel like I need to go to a church to be a good person"

That is what a lot of people stand by in life, that we are good people, but the problem with this is by who's standard though? Our own, the world or by God? it's not church we actually seek, it is Jesus Christ we have to encounter.

No 3 Man – "I go to church on occasion, but I've found it rather boring and irrelevant to my life. I don't mind if my wife goes, but it's just not for me".

These three Men love their wives and kids. They work hard and pay their bills. They enjoy a cold beer and a dirty joke. They're not particularly saintly or sinful. And they honestly believe they're Christians. But church isn't on their radar. They've tried it. It didn't work for them. While some Western men are openly hostile toward the Christian faith, I believe most are simply ambivalent toward it. What's more troubling, the men who do go to church seem to become more passive and detached by the day.

Travelling all over Scotland with CVM, I have to agree with the above, the majority of men who do attend church are passive - this is not a criticism, it's a fact, I've seen it with my own eyes. Compared to a full Hampden park or Murrayfield, the men in church in modern Scotland have lost the roar, we have become muted, I would even go as far to say castrated, the balls have been ripped away.

For the church, who are the missing men? Highly masculine men are missing. Studies show that men who are interested in Christianity have a less masculine outlook on life than other men. The church has a reputation for attracting gentle, artistic, bookish guys who are less masculine than average. "Most masculine of all are the men who have little or no interest in religion" Dr Leon Podles observes, "Very masculine men showed little interest in religion, very feminine men great interest" *Why Men Hate Going to Church*

The *Why Men Hate Going to Church* was a life saver to my faith, thanks to my Mother in-law. I would advise both men and women to read the book, a truthful insight into where the church is at in the Western countries. The way we do church has to change, only the Lord can change the heart of the person, but church as to be a place where the all men can feel welcome. A place where the men can be men and the women can feel safe.

CVM do a *Winning Men* presentation, a wonderful Powerpoint tool that any church could benefit from, an insight into all the things men. On one slide, it says that the church is 62% middle class. I remember sharing the winning presentation at a

WILL YOUR ANCHOR HOLD

church, and this slide came up. One of the guys said "I'm a working-class man, but when I gave my life to the Lord, the way church is run and set up, you feel like you morph into middle class". For me, becoming the best version of yourself through faith in Jesus is not about class. What I would say to any new believer is find the tribe that you belong to, a tribe that will embrace you for who are. A common interest helps too, like music, sport, books etc, get around those who you do life with.

With CVM, I now had an office in Aberdeen, again through a good friend, he has appeared in my journey a few times now, and hopefully going forward too. In fact there are two amazing guys who I have prayed with nearly every Friday, we have been doing this for nearly five years, a life saver for any Christian man. Because it is hard to park in Aberdeen, the days I went into the office, I would park down at the beach, with plenty of free parking down there, and the walk to the office was a good one. One day though, I felt the Holy Spirit nudge me to walk along the beach front, and this is what I did, there was many people walking, jogging on the bikes or walking the dogs. Just in front of me there was a lady walking, I could tell she was heavily pregnant, felt the Spirit say that I had to speak to her with a message. Well, I stopped there, stood still, saying to myself, not a chance, she'll think that I am mad.
I watched her walk further forward, and I was still debating with the Holy Spirit. There are steps from the beach front up to the roadside, and I could see

WILL YOUR ANCHOR HOLD

the lady walking towards a set of steps, there was a bench before the steps. Watching her, I mentioned to the Holy Spirit, if she walks past these steps then I will turn around and head to the office, but would you believe it, she stopped before the steps and sat on the bench, oh boy!

As I approached her, my heart was racing and my mouth going dry, I stopped right on front of her, and she looked up probably thinking, who is this weirdo? I quickly introduced myself, saying I am a father of five and reassuring her that I meant no harm. The Holy Spirit had said that this was her first child, so it went like this "Really sorry to have bothered you, and what I am about to share might sound off the scale. You see I am a man of faith, a father too, and God wants you to know that all will be well with your baby, please do not worry about the birth, God will be with you and protect both you and your beautiful baby". After I had shared, there were tears coming down her cheeks, I asked if she was okay, she smiled and said thank you for your kind words, bless you. I quickly left and walked very fast to the office. I was thinking, what I have done? I hope all is okay during the birth and baby is healthy, but I had a peace, and felt that by being obedient to the Holy Spirit, then all was well.

At home in March 2019, I was fifty years old, and thanks to my beautiful family, they organised a surprise birthday for me at the golf club in Alford. It was a brilliant night with family and friends, lots of dancing too, which I still love to do. They did do a cruel thig to me though, the night before we all went to Brewdog for a smaller family celebration for my 50th I thought, they even took photos and deliberately missed me out on them. I did feel annoyed, I actually could feel anger burning inside, I controlled my emotions, but they all knew they had done the job, getting me flustered. They all made for it with the awesome surprise party, thank you.

In May 2019, I qualified as a Personal Trainer, my vision was to use this to connect with the men, middle aged ideally, to help them get fit and hopefully share my faith them. Delighted to be a qualified PT, but again the men are not the easiest to connect with, I seem to be more popular with the ladies. I did have a few clients, but Covid19 put a stop to this, and I ended up with Zoom fatigue too. Currently, I still have a couple of clients, but certainly not enough to live on.

The summer of 2019 was probably one of the darkest, hardest periods for Joanne and I, especially for Joanne, with her health not good, severe back pain, heavy periods, general not good wellbeing either, she certainly was not herself. Eventually the Doctor decided that Joanne would require a hysterectomy, which is a major operation for a woman, and Joanne had prepared herself for this operation. For me, I knew I would have to step up as a husband, father over the summer, and all other things would have to stop or be put on hold, Joanne was my priority. The operation was successful, and

WILL YOUR ANCHOR HOLD

she was able to rest for a wee while, the reason I said a wee while, those of you who know Joanne, will appreciate that she does not rest for long, and being the fighter she is, she was back at it before she should have been.

Now Joanne's womb biopsy results left us both stunned, amazed and truly thankful that Joanne had given birth to five children. When Joanne went along to see her Doctor, he sat in silence before he explained to Joanne that it would have been a miracle if she had one child let alone five beautiful children. The test results from her womb biopsy had confirmed that Joanne had polycystic ovary syndrome, and one of the symptoms are difficulty in getting pregnant, and, as Joanne shared in her own book, we have five miracle children, thank you Lord. Every child is a miracle, made in the image of God.

After what Joanne had been through, I was delighted that she had something to look forward to in October, the family holidays to Turkey, and deep down knew this would keep Joanne going. Well, unfortunately Thomas Cook went into liquidation, and the holidays were cancelled, Joanne was heartbroken, devastated. Thankfully, we managed to get another holiday with a different travel company. There was Granny, Bampa, Joanne and I, four Bain children, as well as Katie's husband, only Hannah and her Husband who could not make it to Sherwood, Turkey. The holiday was special, a wonderful time had by all, a much-needed break for all the family, especially Joanne. I was delighted for

WILL YOUR ANCHOR HOLD

Joanne, she deserved this much sought-after holiday.

My start to 2020 did not get off on a good note, I had travelled to Abernethy Christian Centre, the weather wasn't too great, but I took the chance to drive, it was sunny all the way to the Centre. I had to cut the meeting short due to snow coming down heavily, looking back I should have stayed the night at Abernethy. Driving back home and the roads were disappearing with the heavy snow, and even though I was at a crawl, while going down the step brae, my car started to slide, and I had no control, eventually coming to a stop with a crash barrier. The car was a mess, but thankfully I was fine. I was so frustrated by my choices that day, and knowing that this was car write off number four, unbelievable. My mobile had no signal, but a kind lady stopped to say her house was just down the road and that I could use her landline. While phoning my car insurance company, I was reading the shopping list on her kitchen fridge, well to say I was shocked would be an understatement, yes there were the usual food items, but top of the list was nipple tassels, and various other sex toys. The film *Misery* came into my mind, and I quickly left the house, obviously thanking the lady for the kind use of her phone, but couldn`t get the shopping list out of my head. That day, the kind minister from the Apostolic Church in Alford drove all the way to where I had crashed my car to take me home, good man.

WILL YOUR ANCHOR HOLD

Now 2020, the year the world came to a stop through a Global pandemic called Covid-19, the word isolation came into play, lockdowns all over the earth. It felt like I was living in a sci-fi movie, honestly, I did, kept looking at the skies for the spaceships to come. Tough times for all concerned, and we were no different. My walk with the Lord was strong, and it had to be to get me through these lockdowns and having to wear a mask, I hated wearing a mask, but followed the rules.

Joanne's parents were due to move into their new house in Alford from Aberdeen. Unfortunately, with Covid in play, their move was delayed for ten weeks, and they came to stay with us while they waited for the approval to move. Ten weeks with the in-laws, now who could handle this?! Actually, now looking back it was a memorable few week, all things considered, we all got on most of time. Thank the Lord it was a hot summer, we were outside a lot, our dog Nala was walked off her paws too. Plenty of time to think (probably overthink), read books and watch far too much TV, especially Netflix.

We started 'waffles and the word' on a Sunday, with the family round the table, sharing a scripture or thought for the day. This is where we saw the father in-law being totally vulnerable, and he embraced these times around the table.

My lockdown highlight was my daughter Rachel learning to play the guitar, she is self-taught, and she kept the family going with her guitar playing and singing songs, she even wrote her own Covid

WILL YOUR ANCHOR HOLD

song, which is amazing. On the CVM front, I hung in there with Zoom meetings, although there's nothing like a face to face of course. Churches all over the land going online and reaching a much bigger audience than they normally would.

Joanne and I started a wee Sunday message on Facebook, sharing our lives, faith through social media, we got great feedback too. I had already started my Friday messages; think they've being going for nearly four years now. It all started one day in the woods in Alford, felt the Holy spirit prompt me to share, and have put out a wee message most Fridays ever since then. 2020 was the year we stopped our Alford Youth Cafe meetings too, we were meeting with the youths of the village every other Friday, this was stopped.

We had started a monthly meeting at the Alford Community Campus, family nights, wall climbing, use of the game's hall with badminton, football, general games. This was also stopped, such a shame. Like many, our lives were on pause, 2020 was a write-off, CVM did an online Gathering, by then, many folks were screened out. Zoom was in the room, and I was one who was fed up with it, please don't get me wrong, great tool, but looking at a screen was taking its toll.

What I did do in 2020 was go back up Ben Nevis, since I felt the Lord lead me to go back up after I had a dream.

Here is what I shared on Social Media that beautiful day the 6th September-

WILL YOUR ANCHOR HOLD

BONNIE SCOTLAND

Three years ago, I climbed Ben Nevis with Mr CVM CYMRU.

That day the sun was shining and it's the same today, I`m breathless with the climb, and breathless seeing the beauty of Scotland.

The reason for the climb is because I believe God spoke to me in a dream, in the dream was Ben Nevis, the Scottish flag and my role is working with CVM (Christian Vision for Men).

For the men, I know many live with shame, guilt, hurt and addictions that are destroying them, so the old set of keys are now buried on the top of Ben Nevis, this represents the old has gone, the past belongs in the past.

Believe the Lord is saying to the men of this Nation, come back to Him, all you prodigal sons, let go of the past and come to your Heavenly Father, don`t let addictions , shame, hurt or mistakes keep you in the dark. I'm praying for new keys, that will unlock the prison doors that many are living with, it`s time for the cry in Scotland of FREEDOM.

This week is National Suicide Prevention week, so today at the top of Ben Nevis, I pray over Scotland, that anyone who is feeling this way , will cry out for help, there is help out there, churches, Mental Health groups and a special mention to #manchat Aberdeen.

WILL YOUR ANCHOR HOLD

For the churches in this land, it may seem like we are on the back foot, but there is a new way coming and the new keys will be given to those who seek after the Lord.

Isaiah 43 v19

See, I am doing a new thing! Now it springs up: do you not perceive it? I am making a way in the wilderness and streams in the wasteland.

That day on Ben Nevis will live with me all my life, the forecast before and after that day was miserable, glad I went for it. The weather was perfect, and at the top of Ben Nevis, not a drop of wind, absolutely wonderful.

2020 was the year of lockdown, and everything was at a standstill, not much happening with the men, and CVM.

Then I got a call from my CVM line manager saying he was being made redundant, yes that horrible word again. I knew that all charities were hit through Covid, and CVM had to cut their cloth accordingly. My line manager is a truly wonderful man, a good friend to me and all the team, I was gutted for him, life is unfair. However I also knew that it was coming to me, and a couple of weeks later I got the dreaded phone call to say that I was being released. CVM were so good to me, and they agreed to pay me until 31st January 2021, a kind gesture.

We finished off 2020 with a wonderful occasion, my daughter Hannah got married to her awesome

WILL YOUR ANCHOR HOLD

husband, it was a lockdown wedding, numbers were restricted to twenty. The wedding was held at Logie Country House, a beautiful venue, and what a weekend was had by all. On the day of the wedding Hannah was absolutely stunning, and I shed a tear or two giving her away. The wedding service was amazing, and as a father, delighted to see a Christian wedding, a beautiful couple coming together in the eyes of the Lord.

My speech was well prepared, and seemed to be well received, yet a relief when it was over lol. A good end to 2020, a tough year all round.

Now into 2021, what is happening Lord? What's next for me and the family?

In March I did the Mental Health Awareness first aid course, with Sports Chaplain Scotland, for my role with Banks O Dee FC. The course was first class and really opened my eyes to mental health, especially for the men, who just do not talk about it.

Joanne and I have always had the heart to plant a church in the village, as the Covid restrictions started to lift as 2021 progressed, we finally celebrated our commissioning service at Tullynessle Hall, though numbers were limited with Covid restrictions in place. We started to have meetings in our home as Covid allowed, and our numbers increased weekly, we were bursting at the seams. This did cause a bit of tension with the kids at home, you know what teenagers are like.

That same year I struggled with news that Joanne shared, it was a hard one to hear. Joanne had asked

WILL YOUR ANCHOR HOLD

me to go up to Lossiemouth with her, I had arranged to play golf that particular day, could see by her face that she was disappointed, yet she left the decision with me. I cancelled the golf, knowing Joanne was priority. That day it was pouring down on the drive up to Lossiemouth, we were going to meet two ladies who Joanne had complete trust in. I am not going into deep detail here, that day Joanne shared that she had been abused as a seven-year-old girl, the two ladies were so gentle and compassionate with Joanne and prayed her through this horrible ordeal. For me to hear that devastating news, my heart sank, and I just went silent. Yet what happened to her had made me realise her reactions to life, what had happened to her was not on, and she has shared all about it in her book- *My Journey back to the Shack*. What a brave woman I am married too, for Joanne to share what had happened to her took great courage, and she has encountered many other ladies who have been abused, yet still living with it.

Joanne has healed well, and now she has a spring in her step, she totally relies on Jesus every day, her faith journey is a great example on being an overcomer. After the ladies had prayed with Joanne, one of them said that they could see two huge angels standing behind us. She asked us both to name our angels, Joanne named her angel Overcomer, I named my one Perseverance, and that is who we are, Joanne an Overcomer and I am Mr Perseverance.

WILL YOUR ANCHOR HOLD

Again, in September 2021, we had wedding number two, this time Katie marrying a lovely guy, who only had one downside, that he supports Celtic lol. They were married at Aswanley, which is near Huntly, what a setting this place is in, gorgeous place. Giving Katie away, yep, the tears were back, but joyful ones, and the Pastor who married Hannah and her hubby, was again leading the service, another wonderful occasion. I was panicking at my speech, again I was using a Powerpoint, but I had forgotten the cable for the laptop back at the hotel. Thankfully, a friend found an older laptop, and managed to connect to the projector, and with success too, thank you if you are reading this. A brilliant wedding, the playlist was first class, lots of fun had by all, everyone on the dance floor, great memories.

Both our hearts are to help build the Kingdom of God, we have a wonderful team of people around us, who cheer us on as we look to plant house churches throughout Alford, Ballater and beyond. We are all for the home church vision, more so after reading a particular book called *The Wild Ones: The Pioneer Call of Emerging Voices from the Wilderness to the Frontlines* – below is from the back of the book :

There is a move of God that is stirring, and a remnant has heard the call—wild, radical lovers of Jesus that have been hidden for far too long. Once the burnt out. The outcast. The voiceless and muzzled. Now they arise as the burning ones to release the word of the Lord and fire of Heaven into

WILL YOUR ANCHOR HOLD

the four corners of the earth. They are the carriers of reformation, revival, and unique and undignified movements. They are a generation of David's called for such a time as this.

In The Wild Ones, prophet and worship leader Nate Johnston offers an urgent summons to the wilderness prophetic voices, and a jarring wakeup call to the established church: If we are to experience a fresh outpouring of the Spirit, we must reform!

In this timely book, Nate offers prophetic insights and Biblical revelation that will set you free from the fear of man, bring a fresh download from Heaven, and reveal your place in God's agenda to bring Heaven to Earth!

In The Wild Ones, you will receive:

- Purpose for your wilderness season.
- Direction for your unique, God-given gifts.
- Healing from the pain of past rejection.
- Encouragement to speak truth in the midst of chaos.
- Empowerment to release supernatural solutions in your sphere of influence.

Now is the time to emerge from the wilderness and be the new sound and voice of truth that will unshackle bonds of oppression, remove veils, and set the captives free. - by Nate Johnston

----

WILL YOUR ANCHOR HOLD

This book has grabbed my heart, soul and spirit, Joanne and I are both 'Wild Ones', often misunderstood by established church. Yet in our wildness we are free, loving life and seeing the Lord move, not in the way we thought, the Kingdom belongs to him.

In Proverbs 16 v 9 (NLT) – *We make our plans, but the LORD determines our steps.*

Joanne and I are living this right now, we don't have all the answers, yet because we have so much faith deposited in our faith bank, we trust the Lord, and we both are obedient to the call, whatever this may look like. A Pastor and writer I love is Rik Joyner, he has a wonderful quote, "If you seek to reach your community you`ll also grow the church; but you`ll never reach your community by focusing on growing your church". We at Alford Community Church look to live by the that statement, we want to reach our community by serving the people, rolling up our sleeves and getting our hands dirty, love in action.

We are looking to create home churches, places where people can grow in their faith and be discipled. They can then be home group leaders and disciple others, growing the Kingdom of God. We aim for more smaller gatherings, where the focus is relationship, doing life together, like in the book of Acts.

WILL YOUR ANCHOR HOLD

THE JOURNEY GOES ON

Wow, I cannot believe that I have nearly finished my book, and a friend advised me to finish well, so here goes…

For myself, I have battled with the generational curses, from anger to whatever has gone on before in my family line. Joanne and I were speaking in a beautiful place called St Combs. Before we spoke at the event, we went a walk along the wonderful beach. Joanne, gently prompted me to do business with God and break the generational curses over my family line. I prayed to the Lord to break any strongholds over the family, in the name of Jesus. That day, I am absolutely certain that the strongholds were broken and praying our children will not encounter them.

The most important call on my life, is Husband/Father/Grandfather, to do my best for my beautiful family, who God has blessed me with - they have walked me through these latter years and have cheered me on the faith journey. I love all my children, they have done well in sport, in the business field with Hannah winning Mobile Hairdresser of the Year, Rachel winning the Scottish Cup U13`s, Katie doing well in her career with the Police, Rebecca enjoying life, and finding her path, praying she can fulfil her dreams, and Samuel who at 14 years old is growing into a good lad with a gift for football and doing not too bad at school, stick in son.

WILL YOUR ANCHOR HOLD

Joanne, what more can I say about the lady who drives me forward, and is my helper in every way, I don't know where I would be without her?

Big shout out to my in-laws too, a brilliant couple who have treated me like a son, they have supported me in the adventure, thank you both.

I still have a heart for the men, both in the church and outside. I am currently a Sports Chaplain with Banks O Dee FC, it's early days, slowly finding my feet in the vital role. I love the fact that I get watch a match as well as attend the training sessions, which helps me get to know the team and build up a genuine friendship with all at Banks O Dee.

For the men of faith in Scotland, many are still living in shame, addictions, anger, hiding behind their identity in the workplace. To see a mighty move amongst the men, its time to be honest, we can't live in chains or shame, it's time to put Jesus first, that's how we move forward. The church in this land has to be more mission focused, I know they want to maintain and support the people who come along on a Sunday, it's not easy keeping all the folks happy.

In John Chapter 21 v 1-14 Jesus appears to his disciples, whom believe Jesus is now dead, they have been fishing all night and caught nothing. In verse 4 it says- "Early in the morning, Jesus stood on the shore, but the disciples did not realize that it was Jesus. He called out to them. "Friends, haven't you any fish?", "No", they answered. He said, "Throw your net on the right side of the boat and

WILL YOUR ANCHOR HOLD

you will find some" When they did, they were unable to haul the net in because of the large number if fish."

Many Christian friends call me a 'Fisher of Men', seemingly my gift is being able to connect with the male audience and connecting with them about Jesus/faith. The above scripture to me is like where the church is at in these current times. Even before Covid the church has been fishing on the usual side, now is the time to fish the other side, then we will see a huge catch. Church, get out of the building more often, go to where the fish are at, cast out your nets to a lost world, get into their lives, roll up your sleeves - it's going to be messy, but with God in it, all things are possible.

Joanne and I have laid down our lives for our family, and the Lord, even now we are wondering what is next, things have not gone the way we planned, but as it says in Proverbs 19 v9 – *In their hearts humans plan their course, but the Lord establishes their steps* - Amen.

Even now as I am writing this, we have put our house on the market, we both feel it is the right time to sell our beautiful home, trusting the Lord as we take our next steps.

During the writing of the book, I did not have a title, finally after much thoughts and prayer, this book is called *Will your Anchor hold*. The old hymn appeared earlier in my book, back in my Boy`s Brigade days, when we sang this famous hymn many times, yet back then in my early teens, the

WILL YOUR ANCHOR HOLD

hymn did not have much significance. Now, after facing many storms, and know there will be many more to come, I believe the book title about my life is well named. Yes, Jesus is our hope and anchor who will keep us in the midst of storms. He is the one who is able to keep us steadfast and unmovable in spite of the tides of life. Hebrews 6:19 declares "Hope we have as an anchor of the soul, both sure and steadfast".

At the age of 53, my heart is strong, my faith is strong, my love for Joanne and the kids are strong. I don't have a clue what is next, yet I have never been so excited or at such peace in my life. Joanne and I have just experienced the joy of becoming Grandparents in these last few weeks, Hannah had a baby boy called Hudson. I can't believe I'm now a grandad! I'm really looking forward to pouring my life into his, and maybe one day he will read my story and be encouraged in his own journey.

As I often say when I am talking, so folks, that's the end of my book, but it's not the end of my story. I hope and pray that you have enjoyed reading my journey. Please be encouraged, there is a better way to live and simple faith is the anchor that does hold firm throughout all of life.

Printed in Great Britain
by Amazon